KRAV MAGA

A Complete Self-Defence Training System from Fundamentals to Functional Combat

KRAV MAGA

A Complete Self-Defence Training System from Fundamentals to Functional Combat

Tommi Nyström

THE CROWOOD PRESS

Contents

Preface

Krav Maga is for everybody. *(Imi Lichtenfeld, founder of Krav Maga)*

The principles of Krav Maga ensure it has a strong backbone and every movement or technique should address the principles. This must not be forgotten even in an era when there is generally more emphasis on successfully passing tests and winning higher-grade belts. It is all too easy to forget that Krav Maga is about the ability to defend oneself in life-threatening situations, whereas belts and levels may be said to measure something totally different. The system was built so that people could quickly learn its guiding practice and apply them through practice and repetition until they become second nature.

Applying the techniques described in this book will help you to pick up the skills needed to survive, but you should seek coaching from seasoned instructors who can demonstrate how the principles are combined in training. You should also take advantage of the many online resources and tools available. In the Introduction that follows and Chapter 1 we will dig into the principles of Krav Maga and what they mean in the context of training for self-defence.

I did not grow up in a dojo. I've played sports all my life but only discovered martial arts at the age of eighteen when I was drafted into the military, as all males in Finland are. Every soldier needs to know how to fight hand to hand, so it was clear that learning martial arts was the way to accomplish that. I spent a few years working through ju-jitsu, kick-boxing, karate and judo, including simplified security and military versions of these arts. When I eventually came across Krav Maga I knew at once that I had found a system that was right for me. From the first Krav Maga seminar I attended, I fell in love with the system's straightforwardness and simplicity. The way in which its rhythm combined defence and counter-attack simultaneously answered the difficulties I had encountered before in my combat training. I learned everything I could about its training and philosophy and it really hit home that military close-quarters battle (CQB) training was at the core of Krav Maga. Straight after completing Krav Maga Instructor training with the International Krav Maga Federation in 2000, I co-founded the Prime Fighters School of Self-Defence in Helsinki, Finland. In 2004 I was elected president of the Finnish Krav Maga Federation (Krav Maga Finland), a not-for-profit national organisation created to spread Israeli Krav Maga in the country. In 2012 we started to develop the Finnish curriculum for Krav Maga training, which was first published in 2015. The Krav Maga Finland style is now acknowledged as one of the many practical applications of Krav Maga. We cooperate with numerous organisations worldwide, including the Levinsky-Wingate Academic College in Israel, and play an active role in maintaining the history of Krav Maga in Finland while contributing to knowledge about this simple and effective form of self-defence.

There have been many notable moments in my journey in Krav Maga, but one of the most memorable was in October 2022 when I was awarded the 5th Dan Black Belt by Grandmaster Raphy Elgrissy, 8th dan. GM Raphy is only the second person to have been granted a black belt in Krav Maga, the first being Eli Avikzar (1947–2004). He worked side by side in the Israel Defense Forces (IDF) with Imi Lichtenfeld (1910–2008), who devised Krav Maga, and Raphy still teaches and trains on a daily basis, even in his eighties.

A working life spent in military and private security has given me some insight into human behaviour. I have a saying that everything goes to plan until the random generator called human beings is added to the mix. There is nothing rational when we, humans, feel threat, fear and aggression. Helping people targeted by domestic violence or bullying, when providing security in pubs and nightclubs, as well as when planning and providing security for public figures, has demonstrated that the philosophy of Krav Maga can be applied at different levels from physical encounters to preventing and defusing threats of violence.

I've made teaching Krav Maga, which I also refer to as 'Zero Distance Solution', my mission, not only as a form of self-defence or CQB system but as a guide to life. I'm very blessed to have the ability to teach hobbyists from two-year-olds to senior citizens (Imi Lichtenfeld himself declared that 'Krav Maga is for everybody'), security and law enforcement professionals as well as military personnel on a daily basis. As an authorised use of force instructor, as well as an acknowledged military instructor advising security and military forces in their training and educational programmes worldwide, I have felt honoured and privileged to promote what Imi Lichtenfeld created as the system of Krav Maga. This has helped tend and enrich the flame by understanding its foundations and history, and by integrating it into ways by which 'zero distance' and 'contact combat' (Krav Maga) can solve present-day problems.

www.kravmagafinland.com
www.zerodistancesolutions.com
www.youtube.com/@Krav_Maga_Coach

Introduction

Knowing and understanding how to defend ourselves is an ever more important factor in life. The violent encounters we read and witness in the media every day create uncertainty and fear. No matter how much we attempt to avoid it, sudden violence, whether it is a terrorist attack, gang-related violence or some other antisocial form of violence, is always with us.

Krav Maga was devised by Imi Lichtenfeld (1910–1998). Imi was a world-class boxer and wrestler, and later a soldier in the British forces in North Africa. He gained a lot of experience from street fights in the mid-1930s, when part of an organisation that provided active security for the Jewish communities in his then hometown of Bratislava, in modern-day Slovakia, conducting armed resistance to attacks by fascist and anti-semitic factions. The organisation used hit-and-run tactics and was involved in street fights against multiple attackers. Imi became its undeclared leader. On the streets, he acquired hard-won experience and a crucial understanding of the differences between sport fighting and street fighting. At this time he developed his fundamental self-defence principle, 'Use natural movements and reactions' for defence combined with an immediate and decisive counter-attack in order that, as he claimed, 'one could walk in peace'.

Imi based the system on his own experiences of what worked in the extremely violent street fights against fascist supporters in the streets of Bratislava, and how it differed from combat sports and the traditional training for martial arts. Collaborating with many skilful individuals in what was to become the Israel Defense Forces, Krav Maga become a systemised approach to surviving life-threatening situations.

USING THIS BOOK

This book is designed for anyone interested in learning how to defend themselves. If you are just starting out, it can serve as your personal self-help guide, supported by online resources to give you a strong head start. For experienced practitioners, such as trainers, instructors and coaches, it offers an opportunity to benchmark your approach. You may find validation that others share your thinking, or discover inspiration to explore new methods of training, teaching and learning.

The core purpose of the book is to provide a clear vision and practical skills for self-defence – specifically, how to simplify the learning of complex situations and the complexity of human behaviour through a systematic training approach.

Humans have both psychological and physiological identities, but our minds and bodies are inseparably connected. If we train only the physical side without addressing the psychological aspect, that training is unlikely to hold up in real-world, high-stress scenarios. In self-defence, our primary goal should always be to avoid physical confrontation. It's like driving a car: we're not trying to crash, but if a collision is unavoidable, we need the skills to minimise harm.

Modern cars offer advanced safety features, but ultimately it's the skill of the driver that makes the difference. The same principle applies to self-defence: it's not just about what you train, but how you train that determines your effectiveness.

TECHNIQUES AND PRINCIPLES

The techniques and principles in this book draw on a variety of systems, but Krav Maga brings them together into a practical, endlessly trainable package. A punch is still a punch, a kick is still a kick – but what sets effective training apart is a strong methodology and the consistent application of key principles at every stage.

TECHNIQUES FAIL WHILE PRINCIPLES LAST

Krav Maga was founded on principles. This means that at the heart of each technique is a systematic approach based on a natural reaction to the given situation. Instead of having to memorise and train for hundreds of movements (techniques) to deal with any circumstance, the number of movements that need to be memorised are very few. There are countless situations in which those movements might be applicable and we can't practise in anticipation of every possible case, but we can train in preparation for the circumstances that each of us is most likely to encounter. To make your training journey a bit simpler, focus on understanding, and finding, the key principles in every technique and then using them.

When evaluating how to survive (note, not win) a self-defence situation, there are a few underlying success factors that we'll need to implement in performing the defensive action:

- Natural response: the integration of the startle-flinch response to the defensive and counteroffensive movement
- Timing and rhythm: simultaneously moving out of the line of fire and affecting the assailant's physical and mental balance
- Don't be there: get out of the line of the attacker's movement
- Counteroffensive and outcome-focused performance: 'Lions don't block' (a slight variant on the British martial arts teacher Tommy Joe Moore's mantra, 'Tigers don't block')
- Explosive strength and speed accompanied by well-balanced coordination
- Maximum of four movements in a sequence that may be followed by another sequence, if needed.

Every defensive technique should be analysed from these perspectives, making sure that the trained technique includes:

- The natural response
- Simultaneous rhythm of counteroffensive movement
- The simplest movements to reach the outcome
- Ability to maintain or regain balance while completing the movements.

SCALABLE LEARNING BY NATURE

In the 1980s and '90s there was a huge rise in the popularity of reality-based self-defence, which inspired many books written by professionals with a background in conflict management and how to deal with violence. They all had the same aim of helping people survive violent encounters with a minimum of training time and technical skills. Some of these were highly influential, such as Bruce Lee's Jeet Kune Do (JKD). Another was Krav Maga, which was exported from Israel to the United States in the early 1980s and later introduced to Europe. As of today, there are tens of systems with different brand names.

One characteristic that differentiates Krav Maga from other martial arts is its emphasis on the art's principles, enabling a weaker, slower or less skilful person to overcome a bigger, stronger, faster attacker. It is a system that doesn't rely on strength and athleticism, but on straightforward simplicity, a 'move and fire' or 'hit and run' philosophy, using one's natural response as the starting point of the 'offensive defence' movement, which makes it practical for all. It never hurts to be in impeccable condition, already in possession of strength and speed, but those advantages will develop once you start doing Krav Maga training and they are not essential before you start.

Krav Maga was created to be scalable by nature. It employs a selected response to similar kinds of problems, choosing an intensity and scale taught through applying the principles learned in training. Krav Maga at its best is a learning system that is based on the user's needs.

1 PRINCIPLES OF KRAV MAGA

Two phrases that are often heard from all self-defence/close-combat instructors are 'Use the principles' and 'This is based on the principle'. The key challenge for the trainee, however, is that these principles might be somewhat intangible and their meaning unclear. What the instructor calls 'principles' might be so contextual and wide in nature

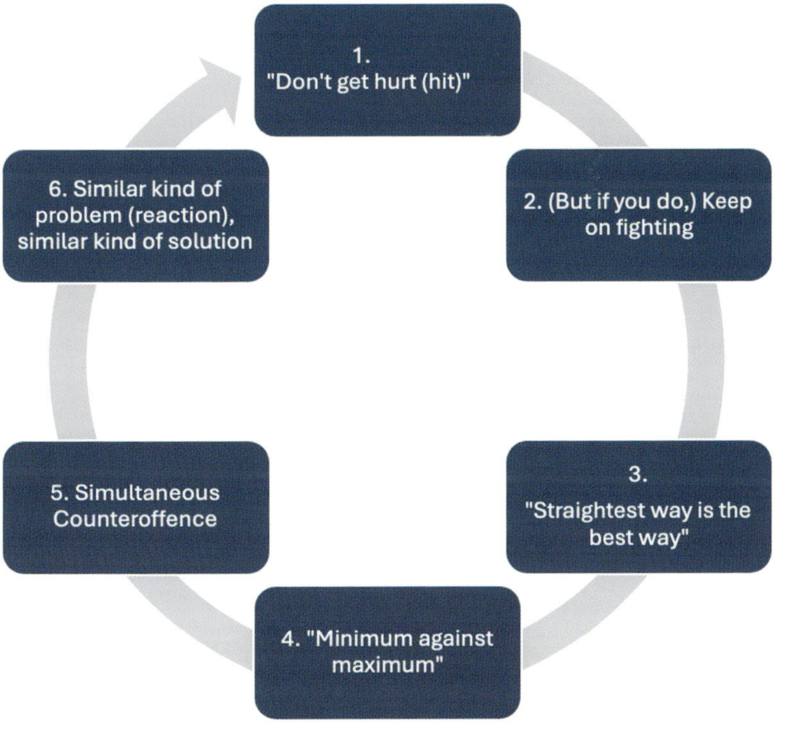

The guiding principles of Krav Maga.

that they can be found in any movement and thus difficult to pin down.

An internet search for the key principles of Krav Maga or other self-defence systems will produce dozens of principles. These are impossible to remember and evaluate. In order to make this straightforward, let's divide them up into the core principles and then explore what subsections or 'descriptive principles' can be added underneath.

Never forget that these are merely the means for evaluating whether a movement is worth training as a principle-based solution (Krav Maga) or it is more of a mechanical movement solution that only works in a demonstration. Let's explore these core principles and what they mean in terms of training.

DON'T GET HURT

The first of these principles states the obvious goal of any self-defence situation: don't injure yourself. It also guides us through your behaviour when practising, pointing out that safety always comes first. We need to find a compromise when performing the reality-based elements to keep the training safe. There is no point in doing the criminals' work for them and getting injured. Accidents and injuries will happen anyway, but let's not be stupid.

The difference between combat sports and self-defence situations in the street is that in combat sport one hit to the head or liver might take you down, but the referee is there to intervene. In real-life situations there is no equivalent. The principle of 'Don't get hurt' could equally be taken as 'Don't get hit'. In a training context this suggests adopting a 'move and fire' approach, integrating our startle-flinch reaction with getting out of the line of attack, accompanied by an attempt to force the attacker off balance (both physically and mentally). I've added the 'hit' part to the principle to make the description even clearer.

This leads us to another general principle about not being there: getting out of the line of the attacker's movement ('line of fire').

This principle also leads us to practising the art of awareness and de-escalation. Just as when driving a car, it is not our intention to collide with anyone and we need to be aware of the traffic situation around us – not distracted but focused. The same goes for being aware of one's surroundings on foot: once we notice a problem, slow down, change direction and avoid the situation. We shall address situational awareness more deeply in Chapter 3.

Another key element of this principle involves practising communication-based de-escalation skills. De-escalation is a huge part of conflict management and must be a part of self-protection training. It is an art form in itself. From the self-protection perspective it includes perception skills, tactical positioning and non-verbal communication skills, while adopting various stances or body positions from which you can be ready to move should the attempt at de-escalation fail.

The exercise begins with the assailant startling the defender, for example by yelling loudly or making her turn around before quickly slapping her to the face. Become familiar with your natural responses in such circumstances. Try different starting scenarios, such as with the assailant's hands on your chest or when holding a mobile phone as you turn around. These help to enforce the body position.

The natural response here is for the head and upper torso to move backwards. Take advantage of this by integrating a front kick to the groin as part of the movement. This demonstrates how a simultaneous attack principle can be added to the exercise.

Once the first attack has been delivered, forcing the opponent off balance, continue attacking with punches.

With the opponent moving backwards, the defender can now decide whether it would be better to leave the scene. Hedi's body posture, however, allows her to renew the counteroffensive with a kick or a punch, if needed.

...BUT IF YOU DO KEEP ON FIGHTING

That brings us to the mentality of survival. Whatever happens, the eventual aim should always be to survive. This is where the mental side of Krav Maga comes into play: however many times life strikes a blow, we still need to keep going.

In training this principle is addressed once we are comfortable in the different aspects of face-to-face combat. It involves striking out from the safety of the comfort zone, discovering mental and physical capacities we never thought we had.

You should adopt the attitude of not stopping until the goal is reached, which can be summed up as 'ABC – Always be Continuing' or '+1 movement'. This requires balance and coordination, physical skills that are key to surviving an event where self-defence is needed or winning in combat or a combat-sport situation.

THE STRAIGHTEST WAY IS THE BEST WAY

This idea can also be expressed as 'the closest weapon, the closest target'. Krav Maga was founded on fast-track learning and usability, relying upon a focus on the initial movement, your natural reaction and the effective use of one's body to stop the attacker harming you. The simplicity of this method can be judged from watching real-life self-defence situations recreated in online videos.

This simplicity extends to the concept that there should be a maximum of four movements in a sequence that helps us maintain our physical balance and 'keep on fighting' attitude, promoted by the concepts of ABC or +1 movements.

SIMULTANEOUS OFFENCE AND DEFENCE

In order to thwart an attacker's intentions, you need to break their rhythm. The original form of this principle was 'simultaneous defence and counter-attack. I have taken the liberty of swapping the actions and changing a word to place the focus on offence, since, as stated earlier, 'lions don't block' and nor should we. Always focus on stopping the attacker's intentions and not on how to block him, since zero-distance survival incidents are never won by blocking. For now, keep this idea in mind as it takes Krav Maga training beyond what is generally seen. Intention drives attention.

SIMILAR KIND OF PROBLEM (REACTION), SIMILAR KIND OF SOLUTION

At the heart of Krav Maga is the principle of simplicity and how to address similar types of problems (attacks) in a similar way. I have added the word 'reaction' to the heading to make clearer the defensive, reactive point of view. This means that in training we must always include natural reactions as part of the 'technique' we're practising. If something is coming towards our head at speed, the automatic reaction is to move it in the safest direction our brain tells it to go. From there you need to find the 'straightest way' to the 'simultaneous counteroffence', thus following the first principle of 'don't get hurt/hit' with 'keep on fighting'.

This can also be viewed from the point of view of active defence (that is, attacking). The person taking the initiative in a combat is more likely to win than the one needing to react. Keeping the initiative is the key

Minimum Effort, Maximum Result

In every circumstance we should always ask, 'What is the simplest way to do this and cut to the chase?' This is a major reason why I call Krav Maga the 'lean process of self-defence'. In manufacturing, lean philosophy is all about simplifying the production process in both materials and methods so that nothing is wasted, eliminating anything that doesn't benefit the customer. This principle of Krav Maga interacts with and brings together all the other principles.

to winning in combat sports. In self-defence situations we don't win, we survive. The key factor in success here is to Distract, Disable, Detain and Disappear. This principle will be explained in detail in Chapter 3.

SUMMARY

To improve your chances of surviving a self-defence situation you need to understand the principles described and tie them to every exercise, by which I mean the time-line of self-defence from detecting the threat, deploying tactics to defuse the situation with verbal and non-verbal communication and positioning oneself to get ready to defend. How we deploy this defence depends on whether we're ambushed, in which case there is no opportunity to detect and defuse, or we have enough time to see the warning signs and try to defuse the danger. We must then decide how far to actively defend ourselves to the 'optimal level of arousal' described by Dave Grossman in his book *On Combat: The Psychology and Physiology of Deadly Combat in War and in Peace* (2004).

Krav Maga training should incorporate all three of these skills. Detecting and defusing are constantly mentioned in physical training, but seldom receive as much attention as the physical side. It is also very easy to forget about the psychological elements of zero-distance encounters, the fear, the anxiety and the aggression, and what all these emotions do to our mind and body. This leads us to the next chapter where psychology meets physiology.

The three major phases of self-defence: detecting the threats; defusing the danger; and, if there is no alternative, defending yourself against it.

2 PSYCHOLOGY MEETS PHYSIOLOGY

In humans the mind and body act as one. When we are fighting for survival, all rational thought flies out the window, so to speak. Our brain is solely focused on survival, while our body carries out motions of which we are unaware. It is these motions that we need to replicate in training under conditions when we are fully conscious about our movements. Understanding how our body works naturally, unconsciously, and then reproducing these same movements consciously is what we call 'doing the right things in the right way'.

Before we dig deeper into the mechanics of Krav Maga techniques, let's consider the kind of reactions we may expect to encounter in ourselves and, just as importantly, in attackers and those who pose a threat. We must learn how to read our opponents and take advantage of any behavioural and physical factors that might become apparent in the confrontation, both our own and the aggressors'.

HUMAN STRESS REACTIONS AND BEHAVIOUR

The key to self-protection and self-defence training is how it unveils the psychological aspects of stressful situations. The cocktail of survival hormones that fill our body makes the sports environment feel very different. The feelings generated in physical workouts or when you are stressed out mentally have their own characteristics, but it is a whole different thing when everything is happening at once. There is a vast quantity of books and studies on this subject, but here I will focus on the effects that fear and stress have on us in a sudden violent encounter and how important it is to integrate this into the technical and mechanical elements of self-defence training.

The human brain can be thought of as having three major layers: the forebrain, the midbrain and the hindbrain. The forebrain controls logic and rational behaviour. The midbrain, sometimes referred to colloquially as 'puppy brain', is all about reflexes. The hindbrain, however, also known as 'lizard brain', is where we go when the survival mode hits us hard. What is important here is that we must understand that in a self-defence situation we do not rationalise, we act, we respond. We respond in the way that is most natural to us in that given situation. If this contradicts the techniques we have been taught in training, the natural response will take control. Since this is common knowledge in close-quarter encounters and combat, it is also of key importance that it is incorporated into our training.

Psychological and physiological effects on human behaviour in high-stress situations

Phenomena	Physiological Effects	Psychological Effects
Startle-flinch response	A fast spike as adrenaline, endorphins and other stress hormones rush in Eyes close and once open again they focus on the perceived threat (tunnel vision) The head moves away from the danger Hands push away the danger All movement is the individual's most natural level (not conscious, trained movement) The term 'muscle-memory' refers to the results of training (physiologically muscles don't have memory, the brain operates through them)	All rational thinking is vaporised All senses focus on survival
Tunnel vision	The field of vision narrows down to a fraction of that normally experienced	The search for an action model based on perception is automated
Impaired hearing	The ability to hear commands lessens The auditory nervous system is impaired as other senses override it	In the event of physical confrontation, hearing is not the primary sense in use When in hiding, however, hearing might be the dominant sense, accompanied by smell
Loss of fine motor skills	Blood circulation focuses on pumping blood to larger muscle groups Fingers and toes feel numb as very little blood is supplied to their muscles Limbs don't necessarily bleed even when struck or cut	Reduced sense of pain
Heavy breathing	Regardless of your physical condition, the 'fear-spike' will fasten the heartbeat and cause heavy breathing	All the phenomena above become more pronounced
Difficulty talking	As the major arteries pump blood at a faster rate, the vocal cords become compressed This causes the voice to stutter and quaver	Only phrases that have been practised are available Ability to hold an intelligent discussion becomes non-existent
Difficulty making decisions	Primal movements only Some previously unknown movement models may emerge	Our thoughts start to wander While stress can sometimes impair memory, it can also enhance it, particularly about emotionally charged events

If you want to learn more about the psychology of combat, I would strongly recommend Dave Grossman's books *On Killing: The Psychological Cost of Learning to Kill in War and Society* (1996) and *On Combat* (mentioned in Chapter 1). Another recommendation is the Know Fear online course with coach Tony Blauer (available at www.knowfearnow.com), which offers valuable insights into human psychology during life-threatening situations. Here, however, I will describe a few phenomena that might occur in zero-distance encounters and must be allowed for in Krav Maga training.

These effects have an enormous impact on our performance under life-threatening stress, so they must be considered in physical self-defence training. This is hugely important especially when we are consciously trying to learn the mechanics, that is the movements or techniques. The psychological effects must also be allowed for in the postures and movements. This sets Krav Maga training, in which techniques are based on natural reaction and behaviour, apart from other martial arts. Let's examine some of these effects more closely and then learn how to manage them for better performance.

Startle-flinch response

Everyone flinches. This in an involuntary response to a sudden threat. In a fraction of a second, your body freezes, your head moves away from the danger, your hands move to cover the danger and we curl into a ball. We can't unlearn this reaction; it is part of our biological defence system. That's why we need to learn how to use it to our advantage. This is not often mentioned in traditional Krav Maga training, but the subject is discussed in a number of videos, made mostly in the 1970s and '80s, in which Imi Lichtenfeld, the founder of the art, talks about its principles. Our knowledge of the human brain has come a long way since then, so we are obliged to embrace that in the context of Krav Maga.

Tunnel vision

During times of stress our vision becomes impaired and limited as we try to absorb as much information as possible. In practice this means that when looking at the person's face, we can't see what they are holding in their hands or what the rest of their body is doing. If more than one person or something else in the vicinity is posing a threat we just can't perceive them, regardless of how big these might be.

In Krav Maga we learn where to look when the confrontation begins. Don't look at the person's face or just their hands, but instead concentrate on the chest area. This way you can perceive more and respond more quickly.

Impaired hearing

If you are fighting for your survival, the brain focuses on making us move away from the danger and hearing is not probably the most important sense at that time. It is very important to understand this phenomenon especially in situations that have not yet reached physical self-defence but you need to reduce the aggressor's threat with verbal and non verbal communication skills. The aggressor might be in such a high state of stress that they can't hear or understand what you are saying. We will address the training of verbal and non-verbal communication skills later in this chapter.

Loss of fine motor skills

In extreme survival mode our blood pressure rises in order to keep oxygen flowing more efficiently to the large muscle groups. This means that our body focuses on keeping the blood circulating to the large muscles, causing us to lose fine motor skills such as enabling our fingers to do precise work. An injection of hormones is needed to enhance speed and pain endurance, so the liver starts producing more sugar to fill the need for energy under stress, which can potentially cause the muscles to shake severely. In physical training this means that every movement should be executed sharply and rapidly – that is if it is feasible for the hands to perform them. That is why it is truly a waste of time to focus on the 'angle of your finger' in training. It is also the case that not all the movements that can be performed when the body is relaxed will be available in the event of an ambush attack. Start by focusing on clear, straight, strong movements. As we will find later, the more we can make the training for any action or skill resemble a game the better results we can expect (*see* Chapter 4).

Loss of sensual feeling such as pain

Have you ever sprained your ankle during a team game and simply carried on after a short break. It is only after the game, once the body has cooled down, that we have found that walking hurts. That's what adrenaline and other pain-endurance hormones can do for us. When we discuss self-defence techniques that cause 'pain', we are talking about a feeling that warns us to stop now or there will be damage. It might not be possible to avoid damage in a physical confrontation, and so our body releases pain-endurance hormones to keep us operating. In training we must focus on movements that will not only cause pain but, if done with full force, will also cause bodily damage. We will address this later in Chapter 4.

Respiratory system

In order to provide the oxygen needed to keep blood flowing to the muscles the breathing rate increases. As the system prepares to survive the confrontation, muscles shake, fists clench and 'eyes burn like a charging bull'. This puts a heavy strain on our respiratory system. In Krav Maga training the primary aim is to be able to end a confrontation in a matter of seconds. This requires the ability to be fast, accurate and strong for a few seconds at a time. This means focusing on speed-strength and strength-endurance training. As Krav Maga is for everyone, the level of the physical load should be set to suit the individual. This will be addressed in more detail in Chapter 4.

Difficulty in making decisions

When in a high-stress situation we don't rationalise, we act. With training, however, we can create models that enhance decision-making. These should concentrate on us getting away from the situation before we are cornered and being able to verbalise our communications in the face of verbal threats. At the same time we must train how to position ourselves and learn when there will be no more talk but only action. These are all still conscious decisions that we should train for in a 'game-like' environment (*see* Chapter 4).

When we are practising responses to sudden attacks, we are dealing with unconscious, natural decision-making. This is where Krav Maga training excelled, especially when it was exported from Israel in the 1980s and '90s. Admittedly in the last couple of decades there has been less emphasis on the overall presentation of the techniques and how to repeat the outcome through Krav Maga's basis in natural human behaviour, and more on small, technical details and emphasising the 'correct way' of executing a move. This is more of a pedagogic problem than a technical one. The reality, though, is that no matter how many times we repeat a technique, it only works if it is aligned with our natural instincts at the particular moment. There is currently a somewhat heated discussion about this topic online. It often relates to an individual technique, but seen in a wider context it is more about how to train so that practice routines are relevant to real-life situations. This topic will be discussed in more depth in Chapter 4.

DEALING WITH FEAR, AGGRESSION AND STRESS

Now that we know how our body is affected by fear, aggression and stress, let's learn how to manage those responses, especially our heartbeat. The key to this is rhythmic breathing. We all know about being told to 'take a deep breath' or 'take a deep breath and count to ten' before acting or responding. There is a lot of truth in these traditional sayings, but how do we do this in real life when faced by an individual behaving aggressively or surrounded by a group acting similarly?

Abdominal respiration

When we are startled, we sense a sudden shock all through our body and lungs, just like we experience when plunging into cold water. The panic attack that we are facing right there makes our abdominal muscles tense and forces us into taking only shallow breaths. This will send us further into shock and speed up the body's collapse. To avoid this, we'll need to learn how to turn on abdominal respiration, starting with a simple exercise:

- Stand upright and breathe out rapidly ten to fifteen times, taking care not to inhale any more air.

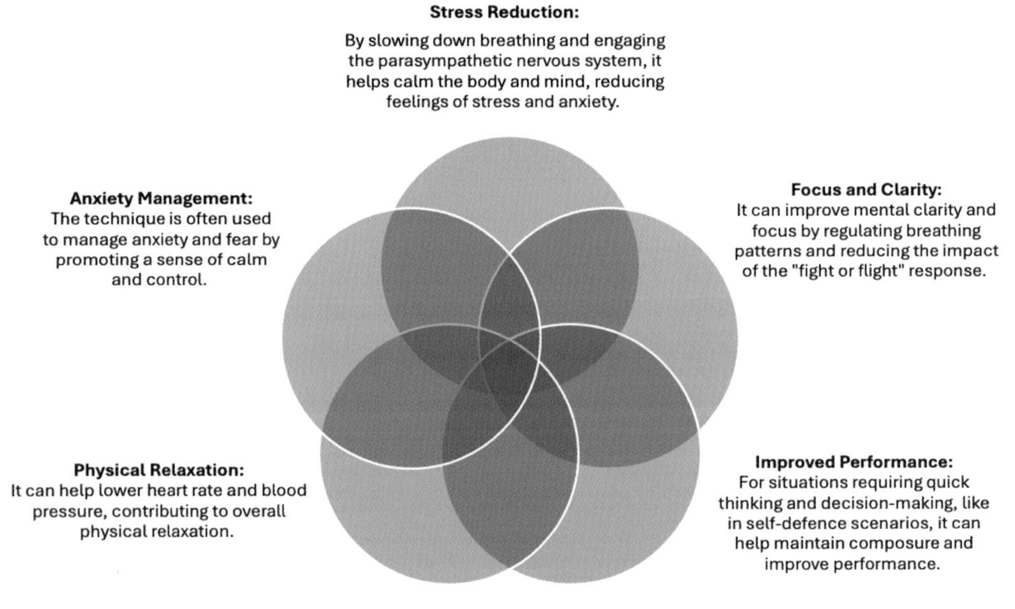

Steps for tactical breathing: 1) Inhale: Breathe in slowly and deeply through your nose for a count of four; 2) Hold: Pause and hold your breath for a count of four; 3) Exhale: Breathe out slowly and completely through your mouth for a count of four; 4) Hold: Pause with emptied lungs for a count of four; 5) Repeat this cycle several times, typically between three and five times.

- Do you feel an increase in your heartbeat?
- Now relax your abdomen and breathe in slowly, filling your whole chest with air.

The same experiment may be done when performing hard physical activities like squatting or making rapid jumping movements. When you're finished, relax your abdomen, breathe in slowly and then breathe out slowly. There are many guides offering advice, and studies have been made on the power of meditation in dealing with stress. Breathing is the most important factor in calming ourselves down.

In his book *On Combat*, Dave Grossman introduced the term 'tactical breathing'. Also known as 'box breathing', this is a structured breathing technique used to manage stress and regain focus by regulating breathing patterns. It involves inhaling, holding, exhaling, and holding again, each for a specific count, typically four seconds. This technique helps activate the parasympathetic nervous system, promoting relaxation and reducing the effects of the sympathetic nervous system's 'fight or flight' response.

Self-assurance

Simple words of assurance like 'You can do this. You can do this. Take it easy, breathe' are examples of how we can talk ourselves through difficult tasks. In a life-threatening situation the ability to talk to oneself is an important skill. It is also a perfectly natural method, something we do every day when we try to remember things like passwords. We can also use similar phrases to communicate with others in heated situations. 'Let's take it easy' and 'Sorry, I don't quite understand' can be used both to keep ourselves calm and to transfer that same calming feeling to another.

We must also learn how to read the mental and physical status of other people. We often hear that an attack came from out of the blue and there was no advance notice that someone would do such a thing. This would not be true if we knew how to read body language. These elements are called pre-fight indicators and to train for them we must consciously train unconscious movements and replicate unconscious behaviour. This is something that has not been trained for methodically in traditional Krav Maga, but it is the principle of 'act as soon as possible', the concept of taking pre-emptive action. Legal advice states that the first pre-emptive measure we must take is to avoid any aggressive situation, but if it is apparent that it is already too late to get away, we must have the ability to respond with physical self-defence. Let's learn how to read the indicators and train to act upon them.

PRE-FIGHT INDICATORS AND COMMUNICATION

Learning to read the flow of traffic is an essential skill when learning to drive. In self-protection we need to learn to read the behaviour of the person posing a threat and then act upon these cues. We can't expect to read them all, especially when they might all be happening at once, but the subconscious movements at the heart of stress behaviour need to be learned and addressed in training. We will address this in greater depth in Chapter 4.

Verbal and non-verbal communication in violent confrontations

The term de-escalation is often thought of as only referring to talking down someone behaving aggressively, but it is much more than just that. Sometimes de-escalating the situation might need physical intervention, but there have been many occasions when a simple 'Sorry, my bad' would have saved a life. In self-defence both verbal and non-verbal communication play crucial roles in preventing, de-escalating or managing potentially violent encounters.

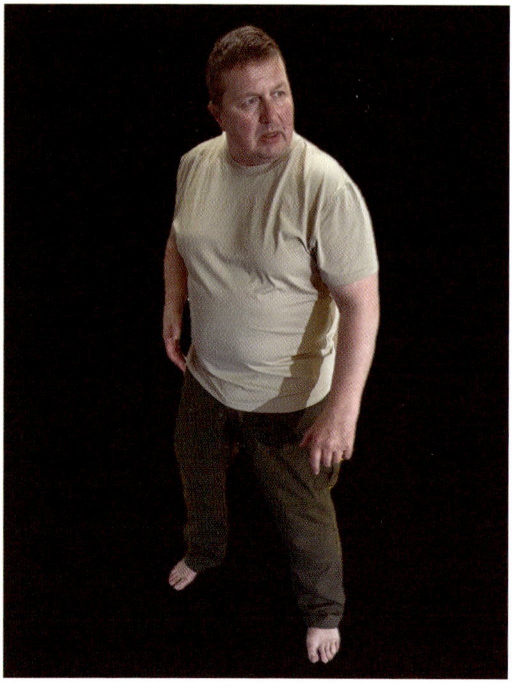

Indexing means that a person is constantly touching somewhere on their body, such as a pocket. In many situations where they have a concealed weapon, this may be where he or she is placing their hand. This is the same as when we quite unconsciously check that we have our phone, wallet or keys. In this picture, pay attention to my right hand.

Under extreme stress people tend to groom themselves. Videos of pre-fight behaviour show that very often people slide a hand across their face, beard or neck, or scratch their cheek. They may also fidget with their fingers, run them through their hair, adjust their clothing or even remove their shirt, in which case physical action is just a second away.

Stretching is a very peculiar movement that often appears in videos where the potential attacker is seen placing their hands on their back or hips or trying to appear taller.

Just as children will glance around to see if anyone is there before entering a room they are not supposed to, aggressors tend to turn their head away from the target before launching an attack. Similar scanning behaviour can be seen when then they are looking around and assessing other people, as though they are looking for someone or judging whether the police are about.

Blading means adopting a fighting stance in which one foot is forward and the other behind. This improves our balance and helps protect our vital organs and stomach area. At the same time we often see the person force their chin and chest forward to intimidate the opponent.

A prolonged, intense stare is a sign of sizing up a potential target or a threat.

In this chapter we will apply what we have learned about human behaviour to suggest suitable strategies to prevent physical encounters, prepare ourselves properly while doing so and deal with any verbal distractions that might be used to throw us off guard.

More than 90 per cent of all communication between humans is non-verbal. Body language, facial expressions and the tone of voice employed are more important than the actual words. The choice of words has a role since they offer an easy target to hold on to, but generally how we say something has more impact than what we say.

If someone approaches us in the street or tries to stop us, we must look for the pre-fight indicators and judge whether now is not the time to be polite but to act confidently, making an immediate assessment of our surroundings and what is happening. We must assume that they might be eyeing us up to see whether we might be a good victim.

Taking the edge off

Sometimes we can see a person looking for a fight. Those around us may be looking at each other evasively or with scared expressions, while the aggressor goes around looking for someone to pick on. The safest course would be to notify the authorities and local security, who are there to deal with such issues, but it often happens that self-help is also needed. In training scenarios we often face a situation where the one playing the aggressor is coming on strong and deciding what to do is a difficult choice. Without a conscious decision this can lead to us starting to back away, repeating 'I don't want any trouble, I don't want any trouble', until we fall off the kerb or end up with our back against a wall. The message we are conveying is that whatever the person is doing is working. We are weak and they are strong. That feels good and sends a dopamine rush through their body.

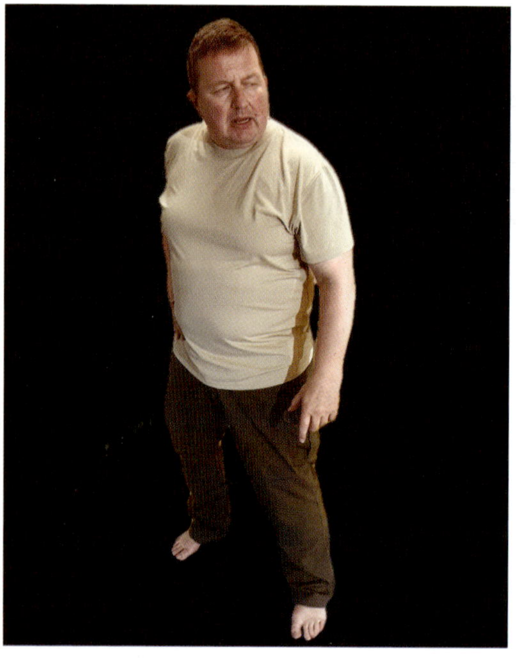

When a potential aggressor is silent their facial expression can indicate that an attack is imminent: tightened lips (to protect the teeth), a clenched jawline (to protect the mouth) and furrowed brow (to protect the eyes).

Hand and body movements indicate the next step towards a confrontation. This may start with pointing and then poking with a finger, clenching the fists, stepping closer and poking the other's chest or pushing one's forehead forward like a ram before a fight.

Let's consider a few strategies that have proved to work to give us a moment to get away from the situation. A person acting aggressively is looking for a fearful response that gives them the upper hand in a situation. 'What're you looking at?', yelled in an aggressive tone and amplified with finger pointing and a forward movement to close the distance, often gets an immediate response of something like 'Nothing, nothing, take it easy, I don't want any trouble.' But what if we turn this into 'Sorry, I was miles away', as we carry on walking away at a tangent while readying our hands to stop any attempt to grab us or hit us. For a different approach you could try something like 'Sorry, I thought you looked familiar, my bad', while similarly preparing yourself. Both approaches take away the possibility of a response like 'I saw you, don't try to deny it', which only prolongs the encounter. In this case our body language also informs the person that they are not getting what they are looking for from us.

These situations are not easy, with stress hormones rushing through our bloodstream instantly demanding us to control our breathing and posture. A calm and neutral facial expression and easy eye contact conveys the message that we are in control of ourselves and the situation. All this calmness depends on our ability to control our breathing. The point is that these situations need to be practised. Just like movement skills, breath control can be practised and adapted to the task at hand.

Stand your ground

If it is not possible to withdraw or move away immediately, or attempts at communication have not done the trick, there is no point in

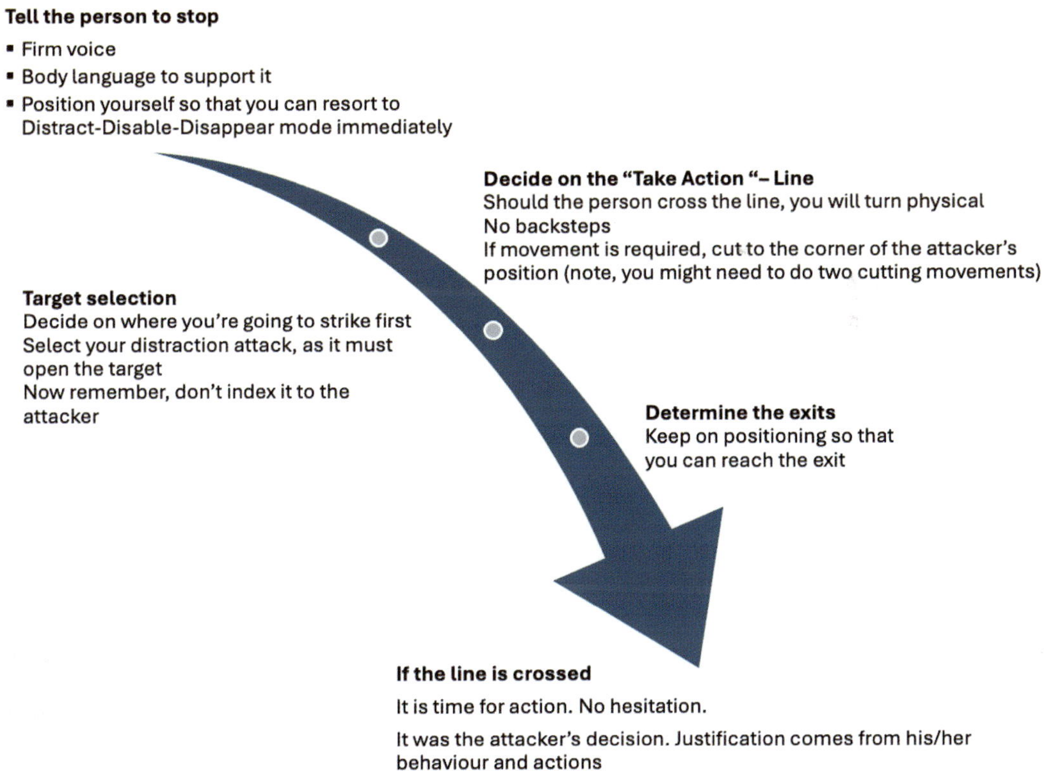

When the encounter starts you should try to get away, but if you are stuck it is time to stand your ground. Establish your defence line, adopting a non-violent posture that leaves you ready to take physical action if necessary. Once that line has been crossed it is time for action.

moving backwards. Once you have learned the techniques, keep this principle in mind, summed up as 'if you try to run away, you'll just get beaten and end up with a sweaty face'. There may indeed be times when fast legs are the best first line of defence, but standing your ground is a winning strategy in all forms of combat and battle. In self-defence situations, however, the law-abiding citizen faces legal, moral and ethical constraints to our actions. That is why we need to practise solutions that will assist in our decision-making. The framework goes like this:

SUMMARY

Training for practical self-defence without understanding how humans operate is an ineffective use of your time and effort. Before we start serious training and become more deeply involved with modern teaching methods and learning aids, there is another area of self-protection we must address: situational awareness.

The same psychological elements are present and we can spot the behaviour of a potential attacker if we are aware of them. Before we can offer a legal justification for the physical force required, however, we must be able to answer the question: 'Why was the use of force necessary and could the situation have been avoided?'

We can do this once we know how people operate under stress and are able to read the signs of immediate physical threat. We can also train for this, working these behaviours into the technical training and creating, or replicating, real-life situations that can be de-escalated with our communication skills, so avoiding the necessity of entering any confrontation.

3 AVOIDANCE AND AWARENESS

The term 'situational awareness' is very dependent on its context. In the context of self-protection it holds the ability to detect potential threats and avoid them before the situation turns into a self-defence situation where nothing but physical contact is going to save you. In a broader sense situational awareness can be determined as the ability to perceive, understand and respond to the environment around us. We must be able to act upon our perception in the safest way, make connections between events around us and come up with feasible and safe solutions.

What this means in practice is that we must plan. There are a number of phases to planning and we must be able to change dynamically from one course of action to another. For any given action there should be a primary, secondary and emergency plan. Always choose the safest course of action. Avoid physical confrontation while preparing yourself to instigate full-speed, all-out aggression, because if the situation deteriorates towards the need for self-defence it is very likely you will need to fight your way out. These situations may be very dynamic and sudden, without a clear start and end. The self-defence tactics employed have to rely on the guiding principles, discussed earlier, that one resorts to automatically.

The word 'tactic' is defined by the *Oxford English Dictionary* as 'an action or strategy carefully planned to achieve a specific end'. When we explore this in the context of self-protection, the meaning of tactics, its plural form, refers to:

- avoiding the situation and
- surviving from the situation as unharmed as possible.

STATE OF AWARENESS

No one can be fully aware all the time. That would mean 100 per cent combat readiness, which is just not possible. We would be worn out in a matter of hours. There are many ways to describe the different levels of readiness. Here are just a few.

Cooper's Colour Codes

John Dean 'Jeff' Cooper (1920–2006) was a US Marine Corps officer and firearms instructor. In his book *Principles of Personal Defense,* first published in 1972, Cooper introduced the concept of combat mindset and readiness.

According to Cooper, it is not martial skills or weapons but the combat mindset that makes the difference between surviving or not. This model has been modified by many and is part of awareness training all over the world. Dave Grossman, amongst other experts, has tied Cooper's colour codes to control of the heartbeat rate (*see* Chapter 2). It is possible to align these concepts together with the associated defensive movement capability.

With modern technology we can measure the heartbeat and correlate it to the state of mind. Sometimes we might use physical exercise to stimulate the heartbeat, but if we are expecting to be startled, the heartbeat begins to increase in the same way as it would with an inoculation of stress hormones. By aligning these two different methods of assessing physical and psychological stress it is possible to devise means of controlling them together. The Cooper colour code is a powerful tool that should be understood and used.

Colour Code	Description	Heartbeat Reference	Defensive Movement Capability
WHITE	Unaware of one's surroundings and events around us Not prepared to take action If ambushed, one will be severely injured or killed	At ease, normal personal level 60–90bpm	Natural defensive and evasive movements Dependent on the level of startle/shock and ability to get away from danger
YELLOW	Sense of alertness Feeling of unease Getting ready to act if needed	Stress hormone inoculation is starting 100–115bpm	Time to turn on the terminator mode Remember: Always choose safety 'Lions don't block' Set the boundary where talk becomes no more talk Breathe
ORANGE	There is a threat that requires attention Getting ready to deal with the problem What is happening around you? How are people behaving?	Stress hormone inoculation is speeding up 115–145bpm	Making tactical choices Expect confrontation, which might be verbal at first Get ready to reply Breathe
RED	You are expecting the problem It will not be a surprise (although you might flinch)	Control your heartbeat and your actions 145–175bpm	Keep on making tactical choices Calm your mind by breathing and/or talking, emphasising every word, calmly, clearly and precisely
BLACK	In some literature, there is also the black state of mind This is often referred to as panic or being totally immobilised	We are not in control any more More than 175bpm Collapse is close	Thoughts run around in circles, repeating movements that we mistakenly think are great Breathe

The OODA loop

The OODA loop is a decision-making model developed by Col John Boyd USAF during the Korean War in the early 1950s. Observe, Orientate, Decide and Act is a situational awareness-related decision-making model that helps fighters to understand the environment and anticipate an opponent's movements ahead of time.

In the context of self-defence or combat all this happens within seconds, or even a fraction of a second. Learning what to look for in an opponent's behaviour is vital. By assessing the pre-fight indicators, we must foresee an opponent's intention even before they may consciously know it themselves.

Observe: Gather information from the environment (opponent's movements, multiple attackers, weapons, exits).

Orient: Analyse context and update your mental model (who is the threat, what's around you, what options exist).

Decide: Choose the best course of action quickly (strike, disengage, draw weapon, escape).

Act: Execute the chosen action with commitment and adaptability.

We will return to the OODA loop in Chapter 4 as it is also a very powerful training tool.

SITUATIONAL AWARENESS FRAMEWORK

To practise this method it is necessary to experience the situations and learn to read the 'traffic'. In regular training facilities designed for physical activity and training, we can usually

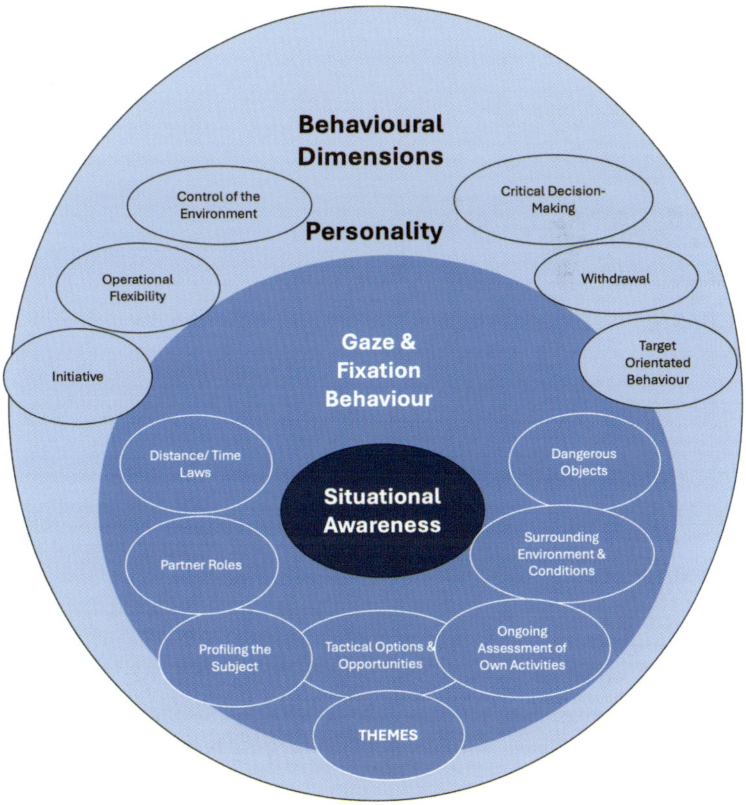

The framework of situational awareness as defined by Juha-Matti Huhta in 'Situational Awareness in Operational Police Encounters'.

only train for physical encounters in locations where there are no environmental constraints such as cars, uneven surfaces or bicycles blocking the movement. Accordingly training of this type must be done elsewhere. Making sure that an individual really knows how to operate in a particular situation requires special arrangements and so this training is not often performed. This is something we have to train for every day by ourselves.

We should start by understanding a few basic tactics and laws that apply in a threat situation when we have not yet been physically attacked. In his dissertation 'Situational Awareness in Operational Police Encounters' (2023), Juha-Matti Huhta identifies seven themes of situational awareness training. It is possible to devise ways of training for these themes that can be addressed in normal physical training environments.

The key challenge is to understand the principles of physical encounters and learn which movement solutions align with the principles in any given situation. By learning to read the traffic we will be able to read the situation, making connections between what is obvious and what is hidden. Understanding behaviour is the key.

Behavioural dimensions

The top half of the chart in the outer ring is about behavioural dimensions. These are different for each individual and so must be addressed as such. There is no 'one size fits all' solution here.

In the course of training we will develop the skills needed to take the initiative and find options that offer operational flexibility and control of the environment where the physical confrontation might take place. It is our aim to find the best way to take the initiative in every situation, whether that means making a getaway, acting upon an intuitive bad feeling and getting to a better location from which to assess the situation, or by addressing and distracting the person who poses a threat so that we can control the environment. One idea is to stand against a wall so that no one can sneak up from behind. Another is to position yourself so that the aggressor is facing the light, blurring their vision. Taking the initiative enhances your ability to make critical decisions.

Understanding the tactics of withdrawal is an integral part of Krav Maga training for both physical confrontation and for awareness and situational tactics training. We must not become too fixated on a single outcome, although this is natural human behaviour. By applying the principle of distract/deflect, disable and disappear, it is still possible to retain the option of target-oriented behaviour in the face of an immediate threat, but once we see an opportunity to flee, we must take it. This also emphasises the operational flexibility and control of the environment. We must train to repeat the outcome, not just the movements or techniques.

Time and distance

In self-defence time and distance refers to the time it would take for the defender to get away, to move to a better location or to respond to the attacker's action, so making the situation better for oneself in general. How you respond depends upon your assessment of:

- Your distance from the one posing a threat
- How quickly that distance can be covered
- What happens when the distance is covered.

Profiling the threat

An immediate need is to analyse the profile of the person posing a threat: their size and mindset compared to the defender; how they move and hold themselves; how they are dressed or what kind of equipment they may have. This may be expressed as:

- Functional capacities
- Mindset and mental state

- The potential attacker's strengths and weaknesses
- Our own strengths and weaknesses
- Any potential weapons at hand.

Surrounding environment

Analysis of the surrounding environment and conditions should include anything that one could use as leverage for defence or the attacker could use to their advantage. This extends to the lighting and construction of the surface. Is it slippery? Is it dark? What can one see and what is hidden? This is especially important when escaping the scene. We must assess and know where we are going, and this is especially hard when we don't know the area. Make a note of:

- The surface's structure, including whether it is firm, slippery or unstable
- How much space there is to to manoeuvre
- The lighting conditions.

Make a note of any opportunities presented by the setting, such as cover and any potential weapons. Once you start looking at your surroundings from this perspective, everything changes. At first it might feel a bit overwhelming, but you get used to it. Car parks will never look the same again once you start thinking about escape routes and where you might need to retreat if a threat arises. This extends to tactical parking, meaning that the car is always pointing directly where you will be going next and you won't have to back out from the parking spot. In the context of going to a restaurant, for example, you might want to think about:

- Where are you going to sit?
- Where are the exits?
- Where is the nearest fire extinguisher?
- Is any first aid equipment visible?
- What can you use as a weapon, should the need arise?

Every situation has its own problems and opportunities. The list goes on forever and thinking in this way will change your behaviour. No, you're not being paranoid, you're being prepared.

Tactical options and opportunities

This covers analysis of the choices that might be available to us that offer a high possibility of staying safe, such as how to position ourselves, how to use the environment in the best possible way, what kind of limits does it place on us and what kind of opportunities does it hold. This assessment must be fast and dynamic. In case we make the wrong assessment, there must always be a secondary plan in place. As a final resort the emergency plan is to attack and fight oneself out of the situation.

- Positioning
- Movement
- De-escalation possibilities.

Dangerous objects

When discussing profiling the threat we mentioned checking for any potentially dangerous objects that might be visible and pre-fight behavioural indicators might suggest whether and from where a concealed weapon could emerge in the middle of the confrontation (*see* Chapter 1). This is not easy, however, while our brain might be occupied in assessing vast amounts of small pieces of information at once.

From Partner Roles to Bystanders

In police work the adoption of a 'partner roles' relationship opens up important tactical choices, including additional resources for assessing bystanders and offering potential outside help in self-defence situations. In our assessment of what to do we must consider what effect those actions might have on the surroundings and any bystanders who are present. What would happen on a crowded metro train or bus, for example, if as bystanders we decide to step in when someone is being bullied? What kind of effect would this have on the bully or bullies, and what would happen around us? When adopting 'partner roles' these are the sort of assessments that must be made before we act. It is the same, of course, in situations where we are the targets.

Assessing our actions

For every action, there is reaction. This is where the system of primary, secondary and emergency planning comes into play. We must be able to dynamically change from one plan to another, according to the feedback we're getting from the chosen course of action.

- Is the chosen tactic working?
- If not, what option should we choose?

PRACTISING SITUATIONAL AWARENESS

In self-defence training we use the term scenario training to describe the format in which

Potential threat detected
Time and distance: Can she get to the car before he reaches her?
Profiling: What are the potential threat poser's functional capacities, size, strength and mindset?
Environment and conditions: Surface is gravel on asphalt, slippery, not firm.
Tactical options: Get inside the car and lock the doors? Not certain the best choice as might lead to a worse situation inside the car. Lock the car and position the car between herself and the attacker? Feasible, as it gives more time to assess the options.

Fact finding
Time and distance: Ability to move to her right, not to her left. Enough time to distract and disable, not enough time to get inside the car.
Profiling: No change. No idea yet what the person wants.
Environment and conditions: No change. Is there an escape route away from the car?
Tactical options: Verbal communication to get the target person to stop moving, but the threat isn't going away. Can't turn her back on the person to get inside the car. Is there a safe exit route away from the car to go and get help?

various courses of action are present and may be chosen. This term is much misused, however, since many times these training sessions end up in physical confrontation just because the trainees thought that as this is a self-defence class, I need to fight. The phrase that must be at the forefront at these training sessions, however, should be 'Always choose safety'. What is the best course of action to make this happen?

Subconscious to conscious actions

We know already that when we are stressed the mind and body focus on survival. If a training session has been too demanding, we can't remember anything from it. The only actions we learn are instinctive, not those that are prejudged or assessed. That's why it is very important that we learn the details of the situational awareness framework and

De-escalation
Time and distance: Better than before.
Profiling: Still posing threat, not moving away from the car. Need to prepare to defend oneself.
Environment and conditions: Are the plastic bins moveable. Is this a pro or a con? Are there potentially other threats? Note the advantage that the bins would make an unseen attack from behind unlikely.
Tactical options: Options to escape are there but escaping might lead to a worse situation in an open space. Can't get inside the car without the threat poser doing the same. Can the person be lured inside the car while we get away (time and distance)? Do we want to let them inside the car (because of what's there). Choosing the line of defence and its execution.

Defence
Time and distance: Once it's time to defend, do it the best way you see fit. Take the initiative and use the principle of distract-disable-detain-disappear. If your first action is not enough, be ready to continue defending. How long would it take to get to the car, back up, turn and drive away? Would it still be better to move away on foot and call for help?
Profiling: What is the functional capacity of the attacker? Be ready to continue if necessary.
Environment and surroundings: Check for any other threat. Where do the obvious escape routes lead?
Tactical options: Depending on the time and distance assessment, leave with the car or leave on foot?

can walk through it at our own pace until it becomes second nature. This takes time and much repetition, always choosing the safest outcome.

The framework itself is very simple, but provides such detailed information that it must not be rushed. The practice can start by just watching videos of the situations, or even pictures, to help recognise each phase of the framework. Before the role play starts it is a good idea to divide into small groups, each with a facilitator, and then the role play starts. As the action proceeds the participant must acknowledge each part of the framework as it arises. At any time they can call 'cut', especially when they feel they are about to resort to physical force. In these role plays the target-person must not take the initiative in attacking. The training at this phase is all about observation, orientation, decision and actions (the OODA loop), not physical confrontation.

All-in action role play

Once we have trained the mind and acquired the skills to deal with violent encounters, these can be added to the role play. Safety is a high priority in these sessions, so you should use protective gear and make sure that the training environment is safe. Any scenario can be chosen as the basis of the workshop. It is helpful to video the performance so that it can later be assessed. The performance should be repeated with the same scenario enough times until the participant has a clear understanding of what kind of behaviour needs to be strengthened and what diminished.

This takes us back to the individual stages of the situational awareness framework. The scenario acted out here is what could happen as you return to your car after work.

SUMMARY

Now that we have investigated the principles, psychology and physiology of self-defence, and discussed how to be aware and prepared for what may happen, we'll now move on to how to train effectively. This will require drawing upon all these factors. In the next chapter we will explore teaching methods and then move on to training methodologies that will greatly enlarge our skills. There have been some recent innovations in teaching techniques that all Krav Maga practitioners should take advantage of.

4 TRAINING EFFECTIVELY

There is constant discussion about the comparative effectiveness of the various techniques. People are looking for simple, technical solutions to highly versatile and dynamic behavioural situations. It is sad to see how these highly complex situations are being over-simplified, putting the focus on whether something being taught is right or wrong, while objectively these are just approaches from different angles.

ANALYSIS OF SURVIVING SELF-DEFENCE SITUATIONS

Looking at real-life videos of different violent situations one can easily conclude that they are not the same. Sometimes we see very aggressive and intense attacks, while others show an attacker being quickly demoralised when taken by surprise as his/her target starts fighting back. The most common theme, however, is that solutions are never clinical and clean. The emotional side of human beings is highly involved in every situation. There are some key qualities that should clearly be present if we are to survive such situations: initiative, a focus on attention, rhythm, a well-balanced body and an appropriate mindset.

When it comes to the combat mindset, the ability to shift from low to high gear while controlling the situation is a very important skill. You should learn how to overcome the results of the rapid release of stress hormones into the body. Taking the initiative is the key to surviving, yet it is important for the individual to know their limits, so a very important training topic is to discover how quickly can one turn the shock into effective action and take hold of the situation. It will be different in a real-life situation, but smart training will help.

In many video presentations of techniques, we see how the person playing the attacker stops as soon as the defence-player starts to counter them. This isn't how real-life encounters work, of course. If the attack-player is caught off balance by the defence-player's first move and remains so, the defence-player has taken the initiative and controls the rhythm. This means that more than one movement or technique has been performed at the same time. Since for every action there is a reaction, the key thing is to force the actions together, allowing the opponent's OODA loop to 'overheat' so that it never reaches the stages of decision and action.

Something to bear in mind when watching video demonstrations is that the full-speed demonstration differs from the broken-down clips, for example the rhythm of hand defence and attacks. What is very common is that in the fluent full-speed demonstration the attack leads the way, but it is the defence that does this in the broken-down demonstration. The problem lies in the demonstration, not necessarily in the technique. Also pay attention to whether the starting situation, distance, body positions and other features are aligned with what we know about human stress behaviour.

Look at the video:
https://www.youtube.com/watch?v=dw0ZuKT3SyM

One basic truth is that combat loves initiative that decisively breaks the opponent's OODA loop, forcing and keeping them off balance while maintaining one's own combat posture. This applies to an individual, a group, a platoon or to larger forces. Coupling the perception with action leads to success. The training methodology makes the difference.

TRAINING METHODOLOGY MAKES THE DIFFERENCE

The long history of martial arts has extended from military fighting skills to today's styles and approaches. In the military, the role of the all-powerful drill instructor with all the right answers is firmly established. The idea of the instructor being the top performer lives on strongly in the martial arts. This also leads to the idea of there being only one correct technique in every possible case. This is a subject we will return to later.

To think that an instructor would be the top player in the group is quite amusing because no one thinks that the coaches of top athletes would outplay their charges. Their job is to make their athletes shine, not themselves. The coach's job is to understand the game and how their athletes can be the best of the best. An instructor's super-power comes from knowing how to get every student to develop into the best possible performer.

In martial arts the techniques being taught are often compared against each other. If we were to take the same approach with basketball shooting, for example, where the feedback is immediate – a score is a score, no matter the situation, body position or style – the results would be amusing. How to make the ball spin is important, but the methods by which this is done differ from one athlete to another. An approach that says 'When the attacker does this, you do this' is appealing in its simplicity, but how do we understand what the attacker is doing? What is our mindset, how do we perceive the situation and what abilities do we possess to deal with the situation? There truly is no single correct technique. Success comes from applying principles, the laws of physics and understanding behaviour.

This individual ability to solve the problem at hand in the best possible way, given the circumstances, is the leading theme. Let's revert to the comparison with basketball: it doesn't matter how well one can shoot hoops when no one is disturbing you, but it is all about how well one can shoot during the game or a game-like environment. The big question is how to build the training environment to represent the 'game' in self-defence training.

Let's dive deeper into teaching methods and how we learn to move. It is very important to understand how the key theories are learned and every instructor must know them. The purpose is not to dive too deep into the subject but to generalise the approach to teaching so that learning and training the techniques becomes easier. In the next chapters we will investigate three major learning theories used in combat sports and martial arts. The ecological dynamics theory connects to non-linear teaching systems, whereas the information-processing theory represents the linear methods, and the schema theory falls in between these two. This concept of non-linear versus linear is very important in learning dynamic actions such as self-defence or in other contact or team sports where the playground is constantly changing, sometimes in a fraction of a second.

THE PSYCHOLOGICAL AND THE PHYSIOLOGICAL

As we found in Chapter 2, as humans our emotions affect our actions. Let's keep this in mind when we move on to training the techniques and developing the physical skills. The emotional, psychological side and our subconscious actions need to be included and integrated in training and conscious learning. The body positions are affected by psychology and in order to train the techniques it is important that these body positions are replicated. This brings us to exploring the foundations of learning movement skills.

The three pedagogic theories found in teaching Krav Maga and other martial arts and forms of combat training are:

- Information-processing theory
- Ecological dynamics theory
- Schema theory.

The traditional way of learning, the information-processing theory, has been widely influenced by the understanding that the human brain is like a computer, which functions linearly. According to this concept we store movement patterns in our brain and fetch them out to use when needed. This idea suggests that we would constantly make conscious decisions, but as we have seen, when prompted by a sudden event, attack or just losing our balance, our body reacts immediately in the most natural and best way it finds at that moment. What we perceive is how we act. This is the foundation of the ecological dynamics theory. In between these two theories falls the third one, the schema theory.

Within the ecological dynamics theory, we'll find a constraints-led approach, a teaching and learning methodology focusing on combining perception with action. The focus is to solve the task at hand in the best possible way. Our subconscious movements are so subtle that we don't even know they exist unless they are deliberately pointed out. This implies that the brain doesn't function linearly but non-linearly. Responding to what we perceive, not to what we know, is the best option.

This method is rapidly gaining ground in coaching, which means that it is very important for Krav Maga practitioners, and their coaches, to understand how it works. The gap between successfully completing a task in a dynamic situation and focusing on the one correct way of carrying out the technique when there are no performance changes on either side will be reduced when adopting this approach. Compared to the traditional information processing methodology, in which all the movements are phased out and very little attention is paid to acknowledging the psychological, natural factors, these issues are solved with a constraints-led approach and ecological dynamics theory. The schema theory falls somewhere between the ecological dynamics theory and the information processing theory, making it another feasible foundation for teaching. In the next few sections we will explore the foundations of these theories and methodologies. Then we will look at the representative practice design that is part of the ecological dynamics and how to use it in learning Krav Maga.

LINEAR AND NON-LINEAR PEDAGOGY

In the evolving landscape of education, the methods we use to teach are just as important as the content itself. Two contrasting approaches – linear pedagogy and non-linear pedagogy – offer educators different philosophies and techniques for guiding student learning. Understanding these will help instructors and coaches to make more informed decisions about how to structure their lessons and interact with students.

Information-processing theory (linear pedagogic approach)

Linear pedagogy is based on a structured, step-by-step progression of learning. It typically follows a clear path from simple to complex, with tightly controlled outcomes. The outlining theory is the information-processing theory. Think of it as a road map: the teacher decides the destination and the precise route to get there. This method often involves:

- Sequential instruction: concepts are taught in a fixed order.
- Teacher-led learning: the teacher is the primary source of knowledge.
- Emphasis on repetition and practice: students rehearse movements until they meet predefined criteria.
- Standardised assessments: Success is measured by how closely the student's responses align with expected answers.

This model is often used in subjects like mathematics or grammar, where foundational knowledge must be mastered before moving on to more complex topics. In the context of self-defence, however, the key problem comes in the form of the ever-changing situation. Remember how our emotions affect our body position and how the slightest change in the attacker's movement will make us change our approach. The game is in no way linear and that's why we must investigate the non-linear methodology.

Ecological dynamics theory (non-linear pedagogic approach)

Whereas information-processing theory assumes that the human brain is a computer that stores the information that can be retrieved when needed, ecological dynamics theory assumes that a human being solves problems as they appear based on a direct combination of perception and action. This means that there is not just one correct form, a single training technique, that would fit every situation. This leads us to the non-linearity in learning. Non-linear pedagogy embraces the idea that learning is complex, dynamic and influenced by individual differences and context. In this approach:

- Learning is exploratory: students are encouraged to find their own solutions through experimentation.
- The environment is a co-teacher: tasks are designed with variability to simulate real-world conditions.
- Teacher as a facilitator: The teacher shapes the environment rather than dictating exact actions.
- No single correct path: Multiple answers or methods are accepted and valued.

Non-linear pedagogy values adaptability, creativity and individual interpretation, making it well suited for developing higher-order thinking skills and promoting lifelong learning.

Key differences

Feature	Linear Pedagogy	Non-Linear Pedagogy
Instruction style	Teacher-directed	Student-centred, guided
Learning process	Fixed sequence	Emergent and adaptive
Role of error	To be minimised	A source of learning
Assessment	Formative, process-orientated	Formative, outcome-orientated
Learning context	Controlled, predictable	Variable, authentic

The traditional methodology of teaching Krav Maga (and combat training in general) is linear. It provides clarity and control over the movement and learning but misses out on natural reactions and movements of the dynamic situation. It also embraces the teacher as the holder of the knowledge. Currently the teacher-centred and directed tradition of step-by-step guidance is changing under the influence of more dynamic training methods. Instructors are more often being confronted with questions of why and how, and the only feasible answer, which most of us have been handing out for years is, 'it depends'. There is a well-established learning theory behind the phrase 'it depends', and all instructors and coaches need to learn how to use it. The new approach is to use the non-linear teaching model and methods like the constraints-led approach.

As an example, the steps involved in teaching a choke release in the linear way would be:

- The teacher shows a silent demonstration from a few angles at full speed followed by
- Slow-motion demonstrations.
- Then explains in detail what is happening.
- After this the training continues without a partner, practising the movements in phases such as (1) taking a step back, (2) bringing the releasing hand to the neck, (3) then adding the striking hand to the movement.
- This will then be followed by putting it all together and practising by the instructor's count, 'One, two, three', repeated until the instructor is happy.
- All the movements will then be performed together at the count of 'one'. The same controlled routine will then be repeated, this time with the training partner. At no point is any improvisation included or permitted.

In the non-linear approach the instructor might start from the phase where the attack-player is holding the defence-player by the throat, the defence-player's hands are already in the preferred position, and the attack-player starts shaking the defence-player to force them off balance. The exercise then moves on to allowing the trainees to assess the situation for themselves and explore their own ideas. As the instructor watches the solutions the trainees suggest, he/she then starts to put in place the constraints that will bring about the solution needed in the situation at hand. The key idea is the self-organisation and, as I call it, 'experience leading to understanding'.

CONSTRAINTS-LED APPROACH (ECOLOGICAL DYNAMICS)

The Constraints-Led Approach (CLA) is a theory of skill acquisition and motor learning that emphasises how interaction between the athlete, the task and the environment shapes performance. It is based on a direct combination of perception and the action needed based on that. It is important to note that, rather than prescribing ideal movement patterns or repeating isolated drills, CLA encourages learning through adaptation to specific constraints that vary from one situation to another. Using CLA in learning the basic techniques is based on finding a movement solution that solves the given problem. The idea is to invite the trainee to use the solution or technique by putting constraints in place that restrict him/her using other solutions.

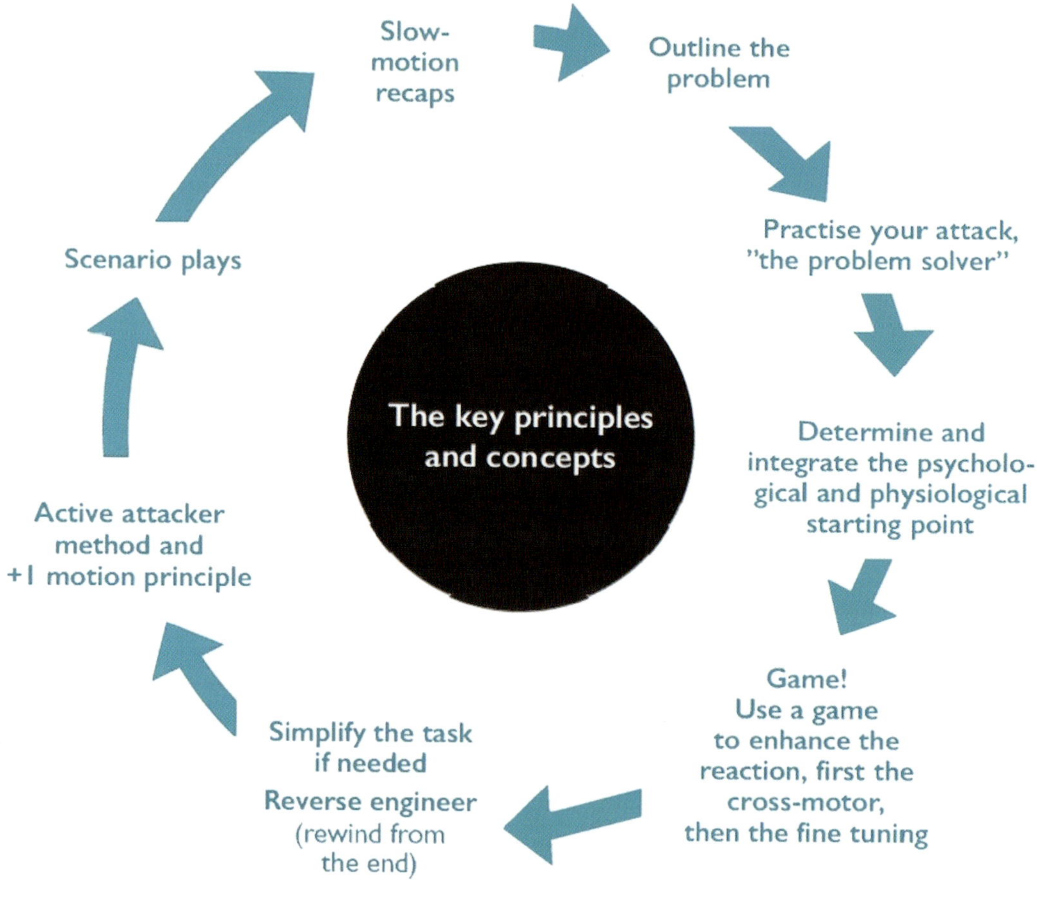

The training flywheel: key concepts and principles.

Nikolai Bernstein (1896–1966), a Soviet neurophysiologist, called this 'the degrees of freedom problem'. The theory is based on the fact that the human body has a vast number of joints and muscles, leading to a massive number of possible movement combinations. This creates a challenge for the nervous system in selecting the appropriate movement patterns for a given task. This is what leads to the answer 'it depends'. As in a self-defence environment, the emphasis should not be on repeating the exact movement but on repeating the outcome. If we want to teach the exact movement that we know is needed, this will emerge if the right constraints are in place.

Key principles of CLA

In my earlier book, *May the Skill Be with You: How to Accelerate Skill Acquisition in Self-Defense* (TMN Coaching: 2023), I outlined a series of measures and tools to enhance skill acquisition and skill adaptation, including the flowchart here which shows how one principle leads to the next.

Instead of telling students how to execute a perfect roundhouse kick, using CLA the coach creates conditions that invite the student to explore and find their own solutions. Here's what that might look like:

- Outline the problem: The attacker is trying to hit you with a blunt object, and you are standing with your head high. For safety, use a soft stick like a swimming pool noodle in case things go wrong.
- Go through the actions of the attack (the problem) and start exploring what solutions might emerge.
- Integrate psychology. The attack-player needs to startle the defender and continue the attack with the next movement.
- Game. The defender needs to stop the attack-player from hitting them.
    a) Constraints: The constraint on the task is that the defender can only use his/her legs for this, and the first attack must come with an overhead strike.
    b) Task: The defender should try to strike with a kick to the groin (make sure a protective pad at the groin area is being worn) while not getting hit by the noodle.
- Simplification. The attacker starts striking towards the defender's rear shoulder, instigating the slipping motion to the front leg side.
    c) if needed, we can return to training for how to execute a roundhouse kick by using CLA tools or schema theory.

Watch the video of using constraints in enhancing kicking skills:

https://www.youtube.com/watch?v=UAkUMS01fUc

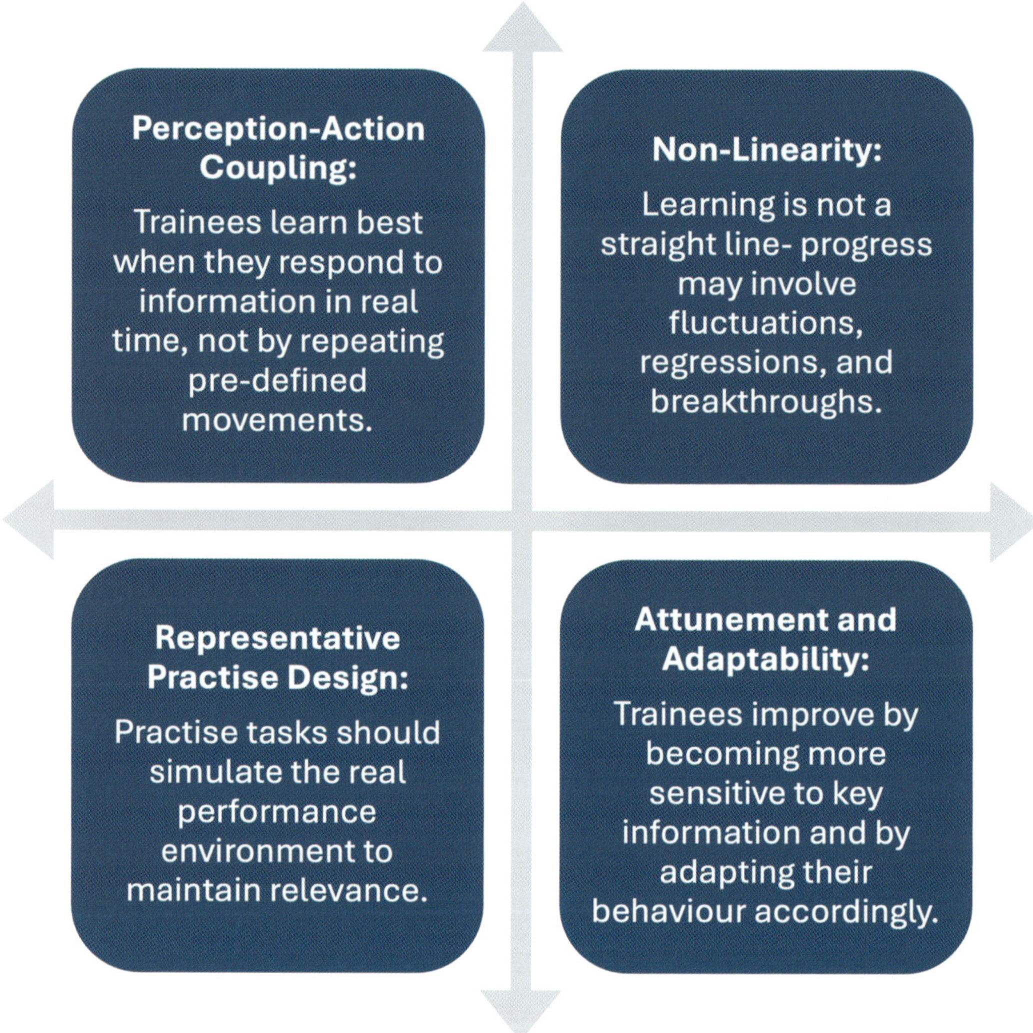

The constraints-led approach develops the tactical awareness as the trainees learn to read the information and the best way to deal with the problem at hand. The model is all about repeating the outcome, not necessarily by always following the same movement pattern or technique. It is all about adapting to actions and direct perception rather than being based on active memory.

CONSTRAINTS

The coach can shape the behaviour indirectly by altering the constraints imposed. This mirrors real fighting conditions, where fighters must read, react and adapt under pressure.

Individual constraints

These are a performer/athlete's personal characteristics, such as height, strength, speed, fatigue level, motivation and prior experience. In Krav Maga training these can be countered with personal attributes such as strength, reaction time, experience with aggression, fear response, injury history, and confidence under threat. In practice this means training with opponents of different strength, weight and size and in each case coming up with feasible solutions to a problem. Size, weight and strength does matter, and one learns how to deal with different problems. We can alter the individual constraints, for example, so that people who are in better physical condition train with two or three others who are in less good shape and everyone gets a good workout. The same approach can be taken to scaling the reaction time.

Environmental constraints

We can challenge our perception skills by altering external factors in the surroundings. Indoors we can alter lights and add sounds and other distractions. By taking the training

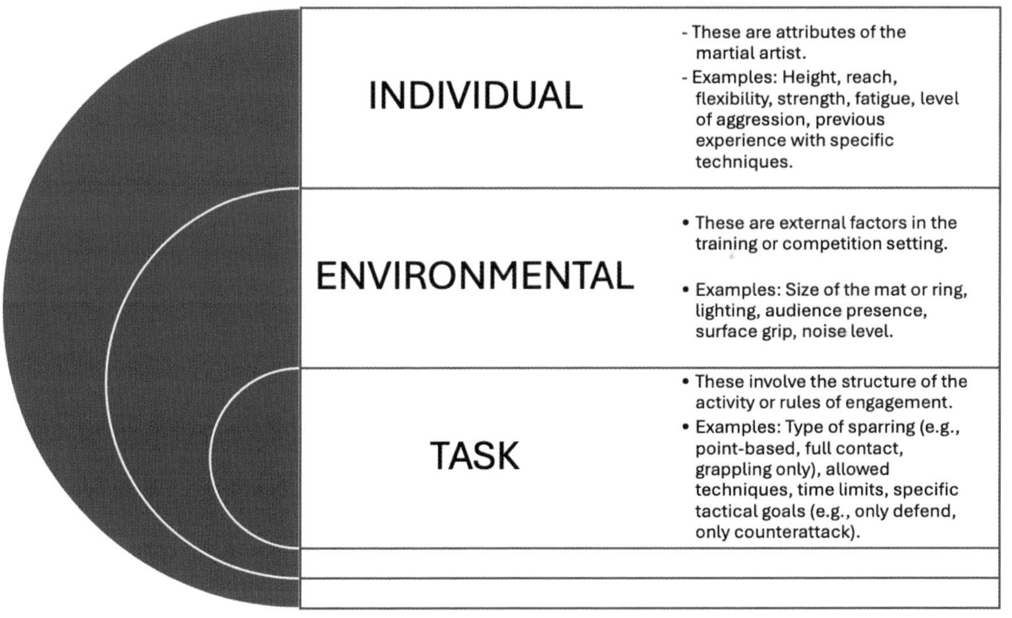

Three types of constraints can be added to enhance skill acquisition.

out to corridors or car parks, for example, we also vary the circumstances presented by the surroundings in the context of Krav Maga. These might include the problems raised by confined spaces, poor lighting, slippery floors, loud noise and crowds, or the features of urban terrain such as walls, cars and street furniture. Training in water or soft sand also provides an excellent environmental constraint.

Task constraints

Task constraints are involved practically every time we train Krav Maga. In order to reach a certain result, it can be approached as a task. This means that every practice can be turned into a sort of game. Task constraints also come with the option of simplifying them. Instead of breaking the movement into small parts, it can first be made easier. Try to achieve the reaction wanted with different stances, leg or hand positions, focusing on completing an easy assignment before varying the attack-player's actions.

Relating the OODA loop to CLA

As discussed in Chapter 4, we need to make a connection between situational awareness and physical training. The OODA loop (observation, orientation, decision, action) is already aligned with the combination of perception and action in CLA (ecological dynamics). In Krav Maga a winning way is to keep the opponent in a state of having to be constantly observant and never letting them move to the decision-action phase. With the OODA loop model we can make the subconscious actions visible and conscious. This helps in using simplification instead of breaking everything down piece by piece, which poses a challenge when learning movements that happen at the same time.

The constraints-led approach is a powerful, athlete-centred framework for coaching and skill acquisition. By shaping learning environments through constraints, coaches can foster more robust, adaptable and intelligent performers, ones who thrive not by mimicking a model, but by learning to respond effectively to the ever-changing demands of sport.

In martial arts, where fluidity, timing and adaptability are essential, the constraints-led approach is especially effective. By crafting training environments that mimic the chaos and complexity of real combat, coaches can help martial artists become more perceptive, responsive and resilient fighters, who don't just follow patterns, but understand how to create them.

Krav Maga is built on principles of efficiency, adaptability and survival under stress, which makes it naturally aligned with the constraints-led approach (CLA). Rather than training ideal techniques in isolation, CLA encourages learning through realistic, pressure-based scenarios, helping practitioners adapt to the unpredictability of real-world violence. CLA trains not just the body, but the mind to make fast, context-sensitive decisions under pressure.

In Krav Maga, survival trumps aesthetics. The constraints-led approach offers a scientifically grounded way to develop functional, adaptable and fast-thinking practitioners by training them in conditions that reflect real-world threats. Instead of correcting a 'wrong' movement, observe how learners adapt within the scenario. By adjusting constraints, coaches can design practice environments that encourage athletes to self-organise and discover movement solutions that work for them. This leads to highly representative and relevant training environments.

Phase	Objective	OODA Focus	CLA Application	Sample Drill
1. Perception Priming	Improve observation of pre-attack cues	Observe	Task + environmental constraints (e.g., noise, lighting)	Partner telegraphs attacks (slow motion); trainee calls out observed cues before responding
2. Contextual Orientation	Train recognition of threat types and context	Orient	Task constraint: add weapons, obstacles, or bystanders	Trainee faces random setups: attacker with/without a weapon, variable intent (mugging vs. assault)
3. Rapid Decision-Making	Practise selecting appropriate responses under time pressure	Decide	Task + individual constraints (e.g., "arm injured")	Trainee must choose action (strike, control, disengage) within 2–3 seconds after stimulus
4. Execution Under Pressure	Build smooth action execution after decision	Act	Environmental constraint: tight space, uneven terrain	Full-speed defence drills with dynamic feedback and physical resistance
5. Adaptive Loop Cycling	Develop ability to reset the loop in real time	Full OODA Loop	Real-time constraint shifts mid-scenario	Trainee starts with one plan, but attacker changes tactic mid-way (e.g., draws a weapon); must reorient and adapt

OODA loop-CLA summary. CLA is a training model for the OODA loop and perception-action coupling can be thought of as the short version of the OODA loop.

SCHEMA THEORY

Schema theory, proposed by Richard Schmidt in 1975, is a cognitive theory of motor learning that explains how people learn and produce skilled movements. It suggests that we don't store exact copies of every movement we perform. Instead we develop generalised motor programmes (GMPs), flexible blueprints that can be adapted to different situations.

In other words, rather than memorising one perfect punch, kick or escape, martial artists build a schema, a set of rules or patterns that helps them adjust their technique to different opponents, distances and timing.

Key components of schema theory

Schema theory describes two types of motor schemas:

Recall schema

- Used to initiate and plan movements.
- Based on past experiences, it tells your body how to move to achieve a goal (for example 'last time I jabbed at this distance and speed, I landed a clean hit').

Recognition schema

- Used to evaluate and adjust movements
- Compares what happened (outcome) to what was expected (feedback), helping refine the schema.

Each time you perform a movement your brain records four things:

- The initial conditions (stance, range, opponent behaviour)
- The movement parameters (force, speed, direction)
- The sensory feedback (how it felt)
- The movement outcome (success or failure).

Over time your brain uses this data to form rules that help you adjust the movement in future situations: this is the schema.

Implications to ecological dynamics and non-linear pedagogy

Variability improves learning

- Practising techniques under different conditions (varying distance, speed, partners) helps develop more robust schemas.
- Example: practising a front kick from different ranges or while moving builds flexible execution.

Feedback matters

- Learners need feedback from both how it felt and from outside, such as coaches or the evidence of mirrors, to refine their schema.

Emphasis on understanding the movement goal

- It's less about perfect repetition and more about understanding the outcome you want and adapting the movement to achieve it.

Schema theory explains how we generalise movement learning through experience. It's especially relevant in martial arts, where practitioners must quickly adjust strikes, defences and tactics depending on the opponent and context. By practising under varied conditions and receiving meaningful feedback, fighters develop flexible, efficient and adaptable skills, the essence of real-world effectiveness.

Comparison to CLA

Schema theory is more cognitivist. It assumes the brain controls movement based on stored rules and past experiences. The constraints-led approach (CLA) is more ecological, focusing on how movement emerges from real-time interaction with the environment. That said, both agree that movement learning improves when learners face variability and must adapt to different situations.

REPRESENTATIVE PRACTICE DESIGN (RPD)

Representative practice design is a principle from ecological dynamics that emphasises creating training environments that closely simulate the perceptual, cognitive and physical demands of real combat. In martial arts, this means designing drills and scenarios that faithfully reflect the conditions fighters or self-defence practitioners will face in actual encounters. The core idea is that the more representative a drill is, the more likely the skills developed will transfer to live contact training (aka sparring), or real-life situations.

Key features of representative practice design

Perception-action coupling

- Ensure learners must respond to real cues (such as an opponent's movement, distance closing, attack initiation) rather than rehearsed or scripted actions.
- Example: instead of 'block on count', respond to an actual punch thrown from a realistic distance and timing.

Information-rich environments

- Include variables such as timing, pressure, range and rhythm that mimic live interactions.
- Example: use dynamic pad holding or live resistance rather than fixed positions.

Contextual relevance

- Design a training session that reflects why, when and how a technique would be used.
- Example: practise defending against a choke while seated in a car, or arrange seating so it is laid out like the interior of a car, rather than on a wide open mat.

Reading the room

- Practice should help trainees become sensitive to body language, intent and timing – the cues that indicate an attack is coming.
- Teaching how to learn to read body language is an important part of the training.

Repeating the outcome rather than a single technique

- Allow solutions to emerge rather than drill a single 'correct' move. Encourage creativity and decision-making.
- Example: provide a constraint (such as only counter-attacks allowed), then allow learners to explore multiple defensive responses. Focusing attention is a powerful learning/teaching tool.

In Krav Maga, where the environment is unpredictable and the stakes are high, representative practice design ensures that training is functional, transferable and deeply connected to real performance. It moves beyond clean technique execution and instead develops fighters who can perceive, decide and act effectively under real-world conditions.

SKILL DEVELOPMENT AND ACTION CAPACITY TRAINING

Before we go further into the techniques, let's define two major parts of movement abilities and capabilities. The distinction is important to understand since otherwise we might think that we are becoming skilled and capable of operating in self-defence situations, while what we are basically developing is action capacity, the ability to perform a movement without any need to adjust it to the problem at hand.

In training Krav Maga it is often misunderstood that an ability to perform something like a roundhouse kick would always be a 'skill'. A movement without external focus, however, is just a capacity to perform a movement whereas the skill is to put that movement into use. We can develop both the skill and action capacity at the same time or separately. In the following chapters we will look more into this, especially when training the techniques.

Why the distinction matters

The concepts of action capacity and skill are related but distinct, especially in the context of Krav Maga and the constraints-led approach (CLA) or ecological dynamics framework. A martial artist with high action capacities, for example being very strong and fast, may still perform poorly in sparring if they lack skill and can't read the opponent or time their movements well. Conversely, a highly skilled fighter with moderate physical capacities can often outperform stronger but less skilled opponents due to better perception-action coupling.

Action Capacity in Krav Maga

Action capacity is something that anyone can do on their own. It doesn't require a group or even a training partner. These naturally help and having a coach to set the exercises and guide the process is a vast benefit. These make certain techniques possible but not necessarily effective in chaotic, live scenarios. The individual capabilities, or constraints, such as strength, speed, endurance, flexibility, reaction time, coordination, balance and mobility, are all attributes we can practise on our own alongside aerobic and anaerobic fitness. Ability to tolerate pain and deal with one's emotions are capacities that are needed as well.

An example of action capacity training is punching without external constraints.

Action capacity in Krav Maga	Description
Strength and power	To strike, shove, grab or break free from holds
Speed and agility	To close distance, evade or reposition rapidly
Cardiovascular fitness	To endure high-intensity encounters
Mobility and flexibility	To roll, fall, sprawl or escape efficiently
Resilience and pain tolerance	To keep functioning under duress
Emotional control	Managing fear, anger or an adrenaline surge

Action capacity refers to the general physical and psychological abilities of an individual that support movement and performance. These are the underlying capabilities that make certain actions possible.

Action capacity determines what you can do, but not necessarily how well or when you do it in context. It's potential ability, not applied performance. For example, the action capacity of a straight punch consists of the ability to use one's hand, hip and foot from a different body position, so moving the target in a different direction than would happen with a hook punch.

Adding perception to action capacity training turns it into skill training, in which action capacity is used to solve a problem.

Skill in Krav Maga

Skill-training requires perception-action coupling. Training skills on one's own is much harder than training action capacity. It is possible to use reaction balls and other sorts of targets, but the best possible training equipment is another human being. Skill reflects context-sensitive behaviour, the smart and timely use of available action capacities to solve problems in real time. Skill is developed by interacting with dynamic, realistic situations, not just drilling techniques statically.

Skill is the functional and adaptive use of action capacities to meet task demands in a specific context. It is how effectively someone perceives, decides and acts in a martial arts scenario. Skill in Krav Maga means being able to solve self-defence problems in real time, under pressure, in varying contexts.

- Reading an opponent's body language to anticipate attacks.
- Timing a counterpunch precisely.
- Applying a choke or joint lock under pressure.
- Adapting to unfamiliar rhythms or ranges.
- Defending against multiple attackers with appropriate movement.

Krav Maga skill (CLA focus)	Description
Perception-action coupling	Recognising a threat (such as a punch or knife) and reacting appropriately
Contextual timing	When to strike, deflect, flee or de-escalate.
Adaptability	Switching tactics if your initial response fails
Environmental awareness	Using surroundings tactically, such as walls, chairs and exits
Decision-making under stress	Choosing actions that fit the opportunities presented in a chaotic situation
Functional movement	Moving in ways that protect you and create an advantage under live conditions

FEEDBACK: THE KEY TO SUCCESS AND FAILURE

Learning is a powerful feeling. Once we succeed, we're delighted and happy. We should also, however, take the same approach to failure. In learning Krav Maga, or any other combat system, we should adopt the attitude of embracing failure and pushing oneself to see how far you can go before starting to fail, not deliberately but simply because your perception-action coupling doesn't yet support it. This ambition to challenge one's boundaries is where the acquisition of skills is found. Failure is as informative a type of feedback as success, if not even better. Let's talk about feedback for a while.

Feedback may be defined as 'Information about reactions to a product, a person's performance of a task, and so on, which is used as a basis for improvement: "Throughout this process we have obtained valuable feedback".'

Feedback is often mixed with vocal encouragement in a clear sign that we accomplished something or that something needs improving. The emphasis is on improvement and that sometimes we just have to keep doing what we're doing, since improvement doesn't necessarily mean that something has to be changed. Repetition need not mean falling into the trap, often credited to Albert Einstein, that 'the definition of insanity is doing the same thing over and over again and expecting different results'.

OUTCOME MATTERS

The idea that there is one correct technique and one correct way of performing it persists in martial arts. Unfortunately this is so even in Krav Maga, which historically has been all about 'getting the job done'. We might find better ways to do things, but it is very easy to forget the context in which they might appear: chaotic, irrational, highly emotional, a mixture of psychological and physical influences, with everyone attempting to do their best. You may spend hours practising the perfect manoeuvre, but reality can slap you hard in the face and force you to complete the task from a totally different posture and mindset. That's why you should focus on producing the outcome and use variations in posture and mindset to develop the 'process'. The example I often cite is how we humans learn to walk: it takes a lot of falling over, and occasionally tears, but we just get up and do it again. Ensure that failure does no damage either physically and psychologically, treating it as something that needs to happen, and you will notice the difference.

Focus the attention

When learning movements we often focus on internal cues such as turning your hip or extending your arm. While our body is performing these actions we can't see them happening. Even though we might think we're

The task here is to hit the pad with a kick so that it turns away at an angle of 180 degrees.

doing them exactly as asked, very often that is not the case. As when learning to walk, we should focus on the task. If the intention is learning to punch a certain way, we'll have to establish the goal. We'll have to establish the constraints, so ruling out some freedom of movement to set the boundaries and then define the aim of external feedback: I want you to hit the pad so that it moves 180 degrees sideways. Altering the position of the pad and repeating the outcome, not the same movement or technique, brings about what Nikolai Bernstein called 'repetitions without repetitions'.

Scaling the success rate

Research on effective learning is a constant topic. It has been discovered that a success rate of 70–80 per cent is a good 'rule of thumb' to scale the demands of the task. I have taken an experimental research approach and concluded that should we fail two or at the most three times in a row, we should allow '10 centimetres, or 4 inches, more reaction time'. This means that we should not slow down the attack but allow our perception-action coupling to develop. If we then succeed three times in a row, we must do the opposite and seek to identify where failure occurs. Another method is to alter the attacker's behaviour so that occasionally there is another type of attack that needs to be dealt with.

Keep in mind that failing must be safe. We must not injure one another in training. There are limitations to reality that we must accept. I will address this later when you will find exercises for each technique and links to videos that will help you create new exercises.

Psychological safety

A key part of learning is to maintain psychological safety around the training. This is easy to say, but somewhat harder to do. As an instructor, or parent, don't focus on the mistakes, but elaborate the successes. 'Do that again' is much more effective than 'That went wrong'. Most of us learn to focus on failures because they are so much easier to recognise than the moments of success. Learning to fail and face disappointments safely is another important skill. In training we're setting up different games and tasks with the purpose of developing skills in a lively manner. These games, or 'scenario training', are a good way of making training simulate the 'game'. Games include winning and losing. Everyone knows the term 'poor loser', meaning someone who just needs to win every time and loses interest should he/she lose. We'll need to address this issue and make losing just part of the game. This doesn't mean that we're learning to give up. We're not giving up, we're getting back up time and again to get the result we want.

SUMMARY

Krav Maga originates from its use by the military. In combat soldiers are willing, able and ready to use violence, some better than others, but the context is crystal clear. Learning in the military is very linear in its approach, but combat changes everything. It is dynamic, chaotic and everything is about combining perception with action. But there is also structure represented by the line of command and the basic tactics by which the battle is conducted. Such principles as the straightest way, the closest weapon to the closest target and don't get hurt, but if you do keep on fighting, are generic to all zero-distance encounters. Fast-track learning and teaching methodologies, however, are dependent on the time available for training and the intended goals. More and more military forces are starting to use the ecological dynamics and the constraints-led approach as their primary methodology. I have been privileged to work with the Finnish Defence Forces and others in changing their approach to zero-distance encounters. Law enforcement and security agencies have followed and it is slowly becoming a norm in civilian self-defence training. There is a very good reason: all these environments rely increasingly on individual decision-making, based on the situation and the individuals in these situations.

There is no single right way to perform a technique. Thus, the aesthetics are less important than the results. There is no need for drilling against an unresisting opponent, while faster learning outcomes are reached by task simplification and other constraints-led approach methods. All training must be as representative of the expected situation as possible. Eventually it must incorporate every aspect of managing the situation, including those relating to psychological and situational awareness. All trainees are individuals who need the best possible approach to learn. This is where non-linear teaching methods score, putting the trainee at the centre with the instructor in the background creating exercises to make the individual a better performer. Learning doesn't happen in the training, it happens afterwards. No matter how good we can get a person to look in practice, what we must focus on is how they perform in a similar situation at some point in the future.

In the next chapter we will come to the techniques. All that we have learned so far has been building up to this. In order to train the techniques effectively, we must learn how to couple our perception with action. Every technique is an answer that comes from combining our perception, body position, state of mind and the attacker's behaviour at that particular moment. Imi Lichtenfeld's advice, 'Be so good you don't have to kill', means that we need to practise, add variations and use the principles subconsciously to make the conscious connection with gaining experience.

5 FOUNDATIONAL MOVEMENT SOLUTIONS

The first part of the book has focused on the foundations of physical encounters, decision-making and learning. This is very crucial to bear in mind once we start exploring the mechanics and techniques of Krav Maga. As a self-defence system based on natural reactions, we must remember that these reactions, body positions, and hand and leg movements are an important feature of the techniques.

Every martial art and combat system consists of the same ingredients: 'A punch is a punch, a kick is a kick.' The differences come from their interpretation, just as in cooking

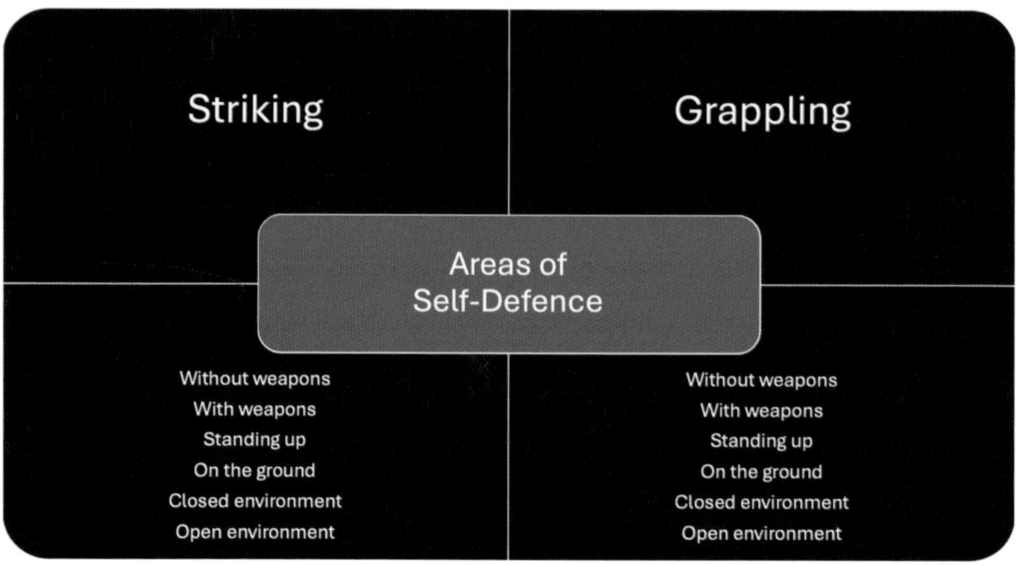

The aspects of physical self-defence can be simplified into striking solutions and grappling solutions. From *May the Skill Be with You* (2023).

one could say that the ingredients may be the same, but the way they are combined in recipes is the cook's work.

In Krav Maga we train techniques of striking with hands, legs and body, from any stance and in any situation. The distance dictates whether we can use the full potential of those strikes or have to also use grappling skills. These are all about affecting the opponent's balance while maintaining our own body balance. The intention is to disable the opponent from action, keeping them constantly in the observation and orientation phase of their OODA loop (*see* Chapters 3 and 4). In the best-case scenario, in which the ability to use one's body as a weapon is immensely important, the situation is over in a matter of seconds. Thus training with resistance and always using the constraints-led approach and representative practice design is the key to a successful outcome of the 'recipe'.

HITTING TO INJURE

The human body is quite fragile. Films and television have led us to believe that it is very hard to hurt a person in a fight, but the laws of physics prove otherwise. Krav Maga is particularly known for its use of the groin kick: the saying 'no groin, no Krav Maga', made famous on television in *The Simpsons*, bears a bit of truth. The groin area, however, is just one of the many vulnerable parts of the body.

Head level

At the head level we have eyes, ears, nose, jaw, the back of the head and the temples. Further down, the neck area itself is very vulnerable with many nerve points and major arteries. The collarbones are a weak spot as well. The throat is a natural target, but we

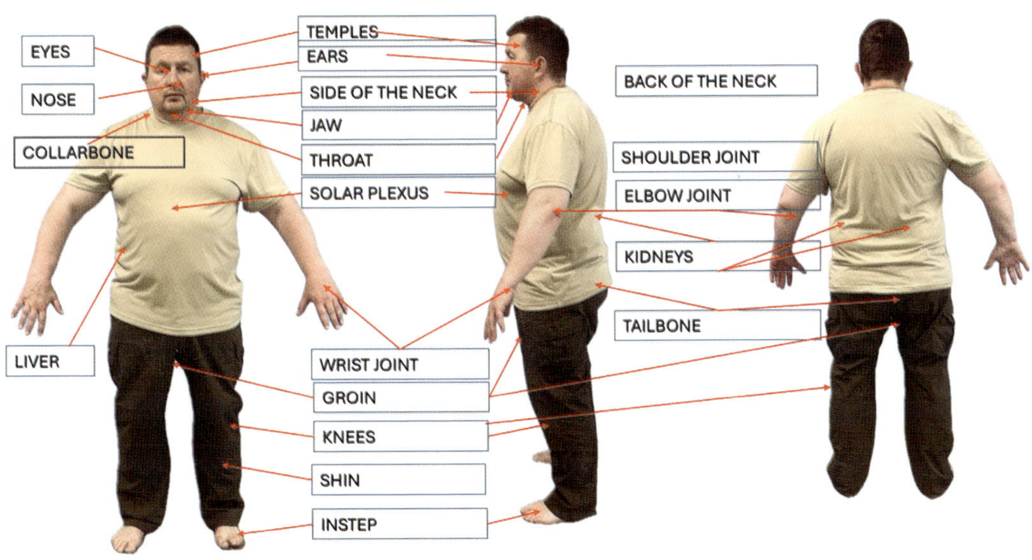

Knowing which are the most vulnerable parts of the body and where to strike is an important part of effective self-defence training.

must understand that learning how to strike there effectively brings the risk of causing the opponent's death and laying oneself open to a charge of homicide.

Torso

The next vulnerable area is below the chest and the ribcage. The solar plexus, liver and spleen are located just around the corner, with the kidneys at the back. Heavy clothing might take a lot of the effect away from striking this area, but physical force will still move the opponent, depending on body weight and the forces colliding on impact.

At waist level there is the groin at the front and the tailbone at the back. Breaking the tailbone will effectively disable the opponent's movement, while hitting the groin area may result in massive bleeding because of the small, sensitive blood veins in the area.

Legs

Further down we come to the thighs and knees. On the inside of the thigh there are major arteries and on the outside a major neural network and, of course, the thighbone itself. Taking out the leg will effectively disable the person so they are unable to stand up straight and will impair the movement. The same goes for damage to the knee. Finally, we reach the shins and feet, where targets are more about affecting the balance than incapacitating the person. However, taking a sharp strike to the inside of the shin may well cause such pain that it takes away the ability to function for a second or so.

TARGET-FOCUSED TRAINING: HIT WHERE IT BREAKS AND HURTS

The renowned expert on self-defence and tactics, Tim Larkin, has formed a whole training methodology around target-focused training, which has always been an integral part of Krav Maga. This involves focusing on breaking the structure so that it affects the attacker's body balance and attention. A kick to the groin, for example, might send out a 'shut down' message via the neural system, but better yet a physical impact below the waist will disrupt the body balance and open up another vulnerable part of the body. In target-focused training the key idea is do the movements in very slow speed. I refer to this as 'slow-motion movie fight'.

The three movements shown here work well together as a chain attack and flow naturally from one to another, leading from a side kick to a hammer punch and then a cross punch.

To illustrate focused training, the three pictures opposite work as a chain-attack.

Legal, ethical and moral problems

Although there is a saying in Krav Maga that there are no rules, the law dictates how we should address the use of force in self-defence situations. While we need to be effective, we must also bear in mind that our actions may lead to legal proceedings if we go beyond accepted ethical and moral standards. This means training to hit targets in a way that will be effective in stopping the attacker's intentions while not killing him/her or, in the words of Imi Lichtenfeld, 'Be so good you don't have to kill'. For example, instead of hitting the person in the throat and breaking the windpipe, hitting the side of the neck will force the body off balance while also disrupting the circulation.

Safety

In Krav Maga the training has always been characterised by aggression, speed and full force. Naturally, we can't strike our training partners with full force to the vulnerable parts, as there wouldn't be another training

Cross punch: using the momentum to strike a powerful cross to create enough distance to walk away.

Side kick: here Hedi is moving beyond my reach and, while doing so, delivers a side kick to my knee.

session for quite a while. People break. The outcome is that there is a tendency to stop the attacks before they hit. Thus we become very good at 'stopping and pulling', as Tony Blauer describes it. However, as was outlined in Chapter 4, by using the representative practice design, describing the targets with focus pads and using protective gear, as well as 'slow-motion movie fight' (aka target-focused training) methodology, we can maintain safety in training, causing full-scale impacts and getting the visual feedback without compromising the effective training. An appropriate saying in this context is, 'if you can't do it slow, you can't do it fast'. This is both powerful and important in Krav Maga training. Even while you are smart about describing the targets and using protective gear, you should still remember that, while a helmet might protect the bones in your face, your neck will also take the blow.

Hammer punch: using the opportunity to hit my jaw as my weight comes forward.

6 BODY BALANCE: THE START AND THE FINISH

Complementary to the actual physical self-defence is the need to understand body balance, how to maintain a calm mental state, and what effects fear, anger and pressure have on our physical capabilities. Practising decision-making and non-verbal communication when getting ready to physically defend oneself makes all the difference to the result, the desired 'specific end solution' of the potential encounter.

When we understand this and carry over all these elements into the physical training, responding to the problem of the attacker's behaviour becomes easier. Every technique is an answer to a specific problem at a specific time. When you are learning Krav Maga smartly, the instructor makes sure that the response (technique) you are practising fits that situation as naturally and easily as the right key opening a lock.

REACTIVE DECISION-MAKING

Far too often we tend to think that 'if I'm attacked with a knife, I will do this', but that approach only leads to us trying to force a 'key' (technique) into the 'wrong lock' (the attacker's behaviour). We will respond naturally, given our mental state of readiness and other factors, to an action provoked by an attacker, but if this natural reaction has not been truly part of our training for the technique, we will have been wasting our time.

For instance, if the technique requires the defender's first movement to duck down or move forward diagonally, and it is trained from a body (and mind) position that makes the defender naturally move his/her head backwards, one must address either the defender's response (the technique) or fix their starting position. That is simple, but not easy.

A classic example in Krav Maga is the 360 defence. What we witness in traditional form is that the exercise starts from the defence-player in a neutral stance with his/her hands down, and then the attacker makes an overhead stabbing type of attack, as if holding an ice pick. The defender is expected to burst forward with hand defence and a simultaneous counter-attack.

This will never happen in real life, simply because it goes against the natural reaction. It is a high-requirement movement to shift from 'yellow' (as described in Cooper's colour code) to 'red' with the attack. In this given

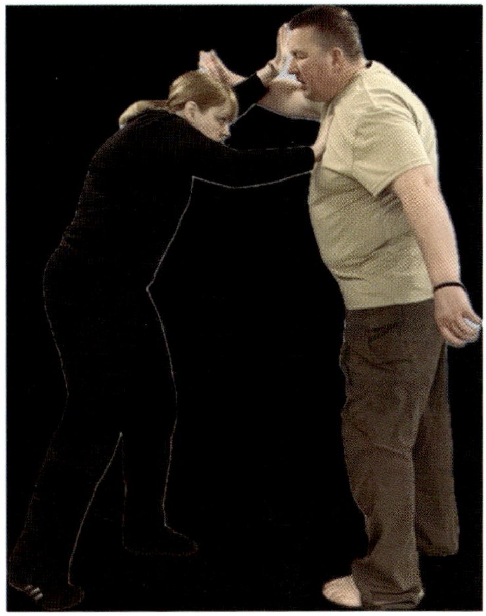

Usual starting position of the 360 defence and its expected result.

A feasible simultaneous attack solution to this situation is a kick and following through with a punch.

situation, the defender's natural reaction is to move her head away from the danger, while using her hands to cover the head or push the danger away. A feasible solution to that change in body balance is to use a front kick as the first line of defence, and then follow it up by re-balancing oneself and continuing with a punch.

This is a classic example of how to take advantage of the natural reaction and binding it together, that is coupling it, with an active defence solution. If we want to activate the 360 defence with the head ducking down, we must change the combat mindset to start from 'orange', or even 'red', and have already decided to make that move. The idea

Hedi's stance shows she is ready for an immediate striking solution.

As soon as the attacker makes a move, the defender is able to respond with a punch.

Four stages of situational training: (1) Adopt a non-violent posture and keep your distance; (2) When it is time to act, provide a distraction; (3) Attack with a kick to the groin; (4) Make your getaway.

is that we are expecting the attacker to make a movement and we will counter that with a punch. The target has already been selected and now if there is a need for a defence, it will come naturally. In the exercise we will need to constrain the situation so that the designated defence action emerges naturally.

In this sequence I'm displaying clear pre-fight indicators. Note that Hedi's posture shows she's ready and waiting for my hand to come up. The decision to attack has already been made (mindset on red). Once my hand comes up, or I make some kind of twitch to indicate an immediate threat, she doesn't hesitate.

This is an example of how to use ecological dynamics in training. It is not about the technique but the outcome, putting the emphasis on repeating the outcome. Naturally, we must learn to respond and attack decisively. The real-life events support the outcome-driven thinking and that's why we must adapt our plans.

PRO-ACTIVE DECISION-MAKING

The other side of decision-making is decisive action. This is when we need to start the attack, for example in a threat situation where the threat-poser is holding a knife or other weapon, and we assess that we'll need to fight our way out. Every action has a reaction, and should we decide to go straight for the weapon the chances are that we won't be successful. That is why it is important to understand that every attack needs to be masked, distracting the opponent's attention as part of the technique.

A basic self-defence exercise in pro-active decision-making takes us from verbal threats to active self-defence. The following sequence goes from making a decision to its execution and then getting away. In this exercise, my role is to play the attacker and I'm showing a number of pre-fight indicators:

- Bladed body position with the lead hand down
- Clenched fists
- Facial expression.

Hedi is playing the defence:

- Deciding on the action line
- Deciding on the target.

Once I cross the 'take action' line that Hedi has chosen, she provides a distraction by pointing with her finger, shouting at me to stop and glancing quickly to her right. It is important to note that she makes sure her distraction stays within the angle of my tunnel vision. The distraction causes me to open my posture higher, providing her a clear route to kick me to the groin.

When it is time for action Hedi moves forward diagonally and delivers a kick to my open groin, since the distraction has made my head and torso move up, making it impossible for me to defend against the kick.

After the kick Hedi must assess whether there is a need for another defensive action, such as striking with her right hand and moving diagonally forward, or whether I am far enough away. Deciding that there is enough room to flee from the scene, she takes off while keeping visual contact with me and being ready to continue defending if needed.

TRAINING TO RESPOND FROM DIFFERENT POSITIONS

The saying 'Make your combat stance your everyday stance' is often associated with the seventeenth-century swordsman Miyamoto Musashi. This sentiment is woven throughout his teachings about strategy and the way of the sword. He emphasises the importance of maintaining a balanced and ready state in every aspect of life, mirroring the principles of a fighting stance. In the tradition of Krav Maga, we can find different 'fighting stances' that were developed by Imi Lichtenfeld to practise different responses to various attacks. These stances simulate 'everyday stances', but they are often mistaken as mandatory techniques that need to be learned. Let's look at these stances and how they should be implemented.

The need for non-violent postures in self-defence is vital. At the same time, however, we need to be ready to burst into action in a fraction of a second and attempt to de-escalate the situation when there is confrontation. Should we be ambushed by an attack coming out of the blue, 'do what you can, but do it right', in Imi Lichtenfeld's words.

These stances serve a practical purpose but very often the hand positions are also found in non-verbal communication when calming down someone behaving aggressively. In the case of a sudden attack, however, the perception-action coupling will immediately take over and the natural response joins the trained response.

It is also important to pay attention to the starting body balance and small details in the angle of the head. Should the chin be tilted up, the head motion will be backwards, making the whole body move backwards. In training this means that there is no sense in trying to fight this natural response. Instead you should move straight or diagonally backwards, coupling that movement with a kick, and then continue to move and fire from another angle. On the other hand, should the chin be tilted downwards, and the heel of the rear leg is off the ground, there is a greater tendency to rotate one's body and move diagonally forward. These are very individual and personal reflexes that need to be considered and notified in training. We can't effectively force a technique, but we can build coordinated responses and, by using the constraints-led approach, refine them by repeating the outcome, though not necessarily with the same movement, since this will change with the perception and natural response.

Inside defence stance

In the inside defence stance the hands are held open in front of you. The palms are open, turned diagonally forward, showing that you are ready to talk and de-escalate the situation, but at the same time ready to respond. The balance point is from the jawline directly downwards to the toes of the front foot, enabling diagonal head movement either forward or sideways. The heel of the rear foot is lifted to provide speed to move forward. The ready state is orange or red, depending on the situation. When asked to give an idea of how it should feel, I use the image of a sprinter waiting for the starting gun. That is the mental image.

Outside defence stance

One of the most natural stances is to place your hands in your lap. In this stance, my front hand is down. As shown here it is across my body, but in everyday life it may well be just down, perhaps from trying to calm someone by moving our hand down. In traditional Krav Maga this stance was created for the purpose of practising defences against straight punches coming over one's hand.

Inside defence stance.

Outside defence stance.

Fighting stance

The fighting stance is not a non-violent posture. Its purpose is to learn how to protect one's head. With a slight change from the hand position in the inside defence stance, we can 'upgrade' to the fighting stance. The biggest change, however, is not seen and that is the mental state of readiness. In the pictures my fists are clenched, but there is nothing wrong, on the contrary, in having one's hands open and ready to strike with palms and fingers, if needed.

Inside defence stance (waist level)

This position resembles those seen in many real-life situations where a person is trying to calm down another by 'talking with their hands' and waving the forward hand downwards to message 'slow down'. When training for a response against a defensive strike, such as a kick targeted at your groin, this starting position helps to enable the movement solution (technique) to emerge. It is a perfect example of the constraints-led approach (CLA).

Fighting stance.

Inside defence stance (waist level).

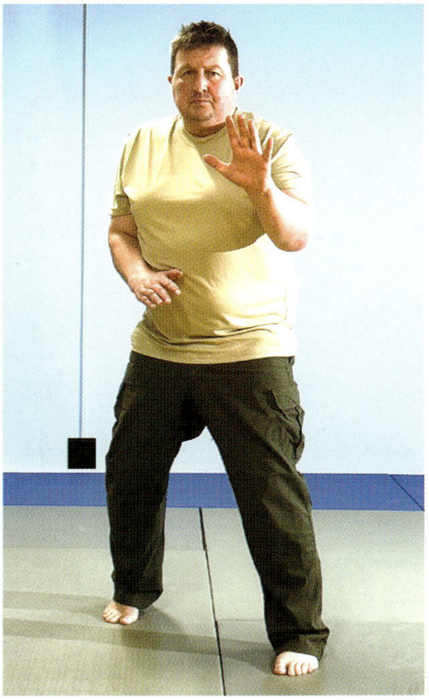 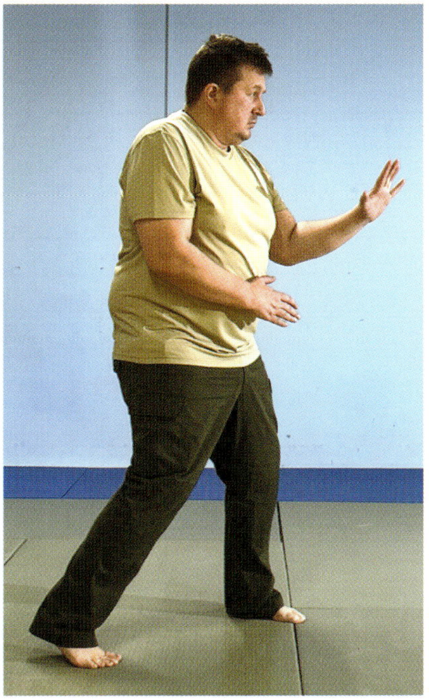

Outside defence stance (waist level).

Outside defence stance (waist level)

Changing the hand positions, so that the forward hand is upwards and the rear hand downwards, is another position that helps certain movements become available. Think of a situation where you have a phone or keys in your right hand and you want to warn someone not to come closer. For training purposes this stance is used when, for example, we want to move and fire with a front hand jab or use a stabbing defence against a kick. We'll get to these later.

TAKING ADVANTAGE OF THE STARTLE-FLINCH RESPONSE

When something happens quickly, we flinch. This is an automatic response that can't be avoided. There is no sense in attempting to lose the response, but plenty in training how to use it to our advantage. One key element regarding the stances is the transfer from condition 'white' in Cooper's colour codes to condition 'red'. Depending on the angle of the attack, this chaotic change involves many small body movements happening at the same time. Once we enter training, however, we are no longer in condition 'white' as our mind is immediately on the alert. Once we have learned how to use the different stances and understand their effects, we are ready to move on to more challenging exercises. This may take the form of starting from the 'neutral' stance while preoccupied with another task, like counting aloud, and then suddenly facing a screaming attacker. Safety in training is of vital importance in this sort of exercise. It is recommended that you start by using pads to represent the attacker and then move on to using protective gear. Keep in mind, though, that protective gear doesn't protect the joints such as knees from bending and breaking. The following sequence shows an exercise that takes you from a neutral stance to defending and stopping the attack.

Using the startle-flinch response from mindset yellow. At the start of the exercise Hedi is focused on her phone and not aware that I'm planning to grab her.

As I startle her, Hedi takes advantage of the startle-flinch by bending her knees, tucking her chin into her chest and placing her hands so as to push away the danger. Note that the phone is still in her hand.

Continuing her attack, Hedi keeps her head down to increase power in her abdominal muscles, using her forearms to hit the side of my neck.

Following the success of her strikes to the side of my neck, Hedi continues with a kick to the groin to create more distance. As a follow-up she could either 'disappear' (flee from the scene) or choose to continue with 'disabling' attacks until I'm no longer a threat.

LEARNING TO USE OUR CORE

When we are forced into a startle-flinch response, we freeze momentarily. As we learned in Chapter 2, this is a very powerful, biological defence-mechanism that we take for granted. In that event of momentarily freezing, our core muscles tense and we might feel that we stop breathing. In order to use our core, the abdominal muscles, to our advantage in this situation, we need to breathe out deeply, but also learn how to activate our hip area to improve our movement. You can click the following links for exercises that help you do just that. These videos will also lead us to the next topic, which is slipping and striking in general. These are not short videos, and you can get a worthwhile training session out of them

Slipping, punching, kicking	**https://www.youtube.com/watch?v=t2UZR-MOUWs**
Slipping and Punching	**https://www.youtube.com/watch?v=AeWblepw1KU**

MOVING OUT OF THE LINE OF FIRE

As one of the key principles of Krav Maga is to get out of the line of fire, the direction in which the attacker is moving, we can establish some general directions of movement, as were shown in the videos. In the following chapter we will dig deeper into these and their practical implementations.

It is our intention to get to the side of our opponent so that he/she can't immediately use their hands, legs or body to attack us. From this position we can attack, fire, and move out or in as needed in the situation. The principle of '+1 motion' means that every movement we make has the next movement already in place to continue. ABC (Always Be Continuing) is another term I use in this situation. This is an example that will reappear in the technical descriptions that will be introduced later. As intention drives attention, bear in mind that we should always try to get to this (tactical) side position when we need to stay close to the opponent. When we are training to find solutions to counter different attack behaviours, we should keep on repeating this outcome. Let us start by looking at the main directions to take when moving out of the line of fire and stopping the attacker's intentions (move and fire).

Diagonally forward with a lead hand punch

In a situation where we expect something to happen, the attacker/threat poser may have closed the distance and it becomes obvious there is no way to escape without physical contact, this is a solution to turn to.

Hedi has here actively decided, not simply responded, to stop me in my tracks. Her lead hand is striking forward while she moves forward diagonally. Alternatively, she could also resort to disabling my right hand while moving and then, if need be, to continue the attack with her rear hand (cross punch). Pay attention to what is happening to my balance as she strikes me diagonally backwards. In order to stay standing upright, I will need to step backwards with my left leg, so making my body's right side turn towards her. All of this happens within a second.

To train for this, it is sensible to use pads or soft balls as targets in order to make the training as representative and safe as possible. You can check out an exercise from YouTube, 'Improve Punching & Inside Defense with Visual Feedback'. Just follow the link

https://www.youtube.com/shorts/VObHhvd-B6A

Start by moving forward diagonally, turning your body towards the opponent, and then punch with your leading hand.

Diagonally forward with a rear hand punch

Another diagonally forward angle is a punch with our rear hand. Usually this comes naturally to the torso (the edge of the liver) and then continues by turning back towards the opponent and continuing the defensive attacking again from the side position. After the initial reaction and attack, the next move is either to the side or to continue with a kick to the groin or knee. When practising we must bring some variety to this by having the attack-player vary the effects of the strikes and provide feedback.

The usual mistake when training for this solution is to start with the hand defence instead of body defence (moving out of the line of fire). Pay attention to Hedi's head movement and how the rear hand (cross punch) is moving forward. The focus here is on punching.

As Hedi's punch lands, it has an effect on my body posture and her defending hand has now moved up to protect her head. What she does next will depend on the feedback she's seeing. If the punch were to send me backwards, she might have enough distance to get away. If not, using her left hand to punch while turning towards me, or delivering a kick to the groin between punches are all feasible solutions.

To the side with a punch or kick

In case your natural reaction is to move sideways to a position from where you can't reach the target by punching, you may resort to either a roundhouse kick or side kick. A roundhouse kick is an obvious continuation when the kicking leg is still on the ground now that your head is already out of the line of fire. As the body defence continues, the kick comes in to send the opponent backwards.

After the kick has landed Hedi here turns towards me making the Slip No. 1 type of movement. She then chooses to push and control my right hand to make room for her cross punch. When her cross punch lands she is now ready to move away ('disappear'), although this departure can be enhanced with a kick – front, roundhouse or side as she sees fit. If the cross punch has sent me so

Moving forward diagonally with the rear hand ready to land a punch.

If the natural response has been to move sideways, it may be best to respond with a kick.

off balance that there is enough distance to retreat without any further strikes, just take off. Again it is important to practise the scene with feedback from the attack-player.

Diagonally backwards with a punch or kick

When our reaction is more backwards than to the side, turning away from the attack, the best response will be to attack with a side kick. Pay attention to how Hedi's front leg is already lifting as part of the movement. This is an important action capacity training movement, joining the knee movement to the head movement. She is taking advantage of the 'abdominal freezing' that is part of the startle-flinch response to load up the attack.

Moving on to the attack, Hedi delivers a side kick to my knee while striking, pushing and controlling my retrieving hand at the same time.

As soon as her kicking leg touches the ground she lands a hammer punch on my chin. This rhythm – 'leg hits the ground; the fist hits the jaw' – rhythm is adopted from tactics used by the boxer Jack Dempsey in the 1910s.

With her opponent disorientated by the hammer punch, Hedi continues the sequence immediately with a cross punch to my open chin to create more distance.

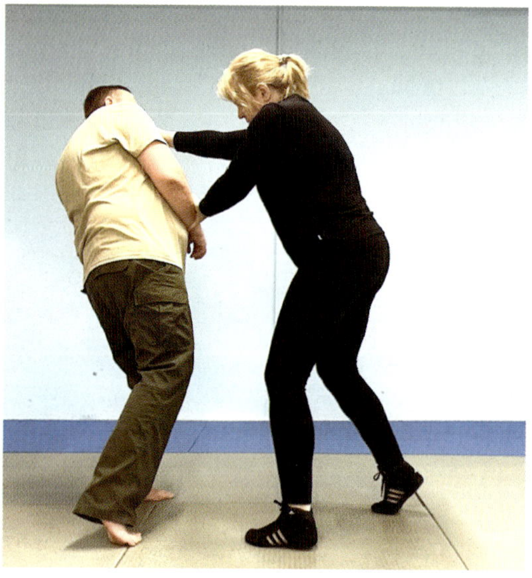

The defence can be followed up with a push and a punch.

When moving diagonally backwards the knee movement can be coupled with the head movement.

Hedi distracts from the incoming side kick by striking and pushing.

The kick is followed by a hammer punch.

Disorientated by the hammer punch, the opponent has no response to a cross punch.

Head-on

There are times when all we can do is to move in head-on with defensive striking. What happens after this depends on our body balance and the feedback we receive from the effect of our attack. This move also happens when we need to turn to attend to attacks or threats from the side or behind us. People often focus on the footwork, but once we start focusing on the outcome, the feet will follow.

The exercise example seen here starts with the defender standing with her back to the offence-player, with her hands on her chest. When she turns to face the attacker she needs to defend as the offence-player is trying to grab hold of her. Using the startle-flinch response to cover her head, the defence-player drives forward to punch with the double elbows, keeping her head covered.

The next phase would be to strike with both fists to the neck area and drive the opponent downwards. A kick to the groin might then disable the attacker, making it possible to escape.

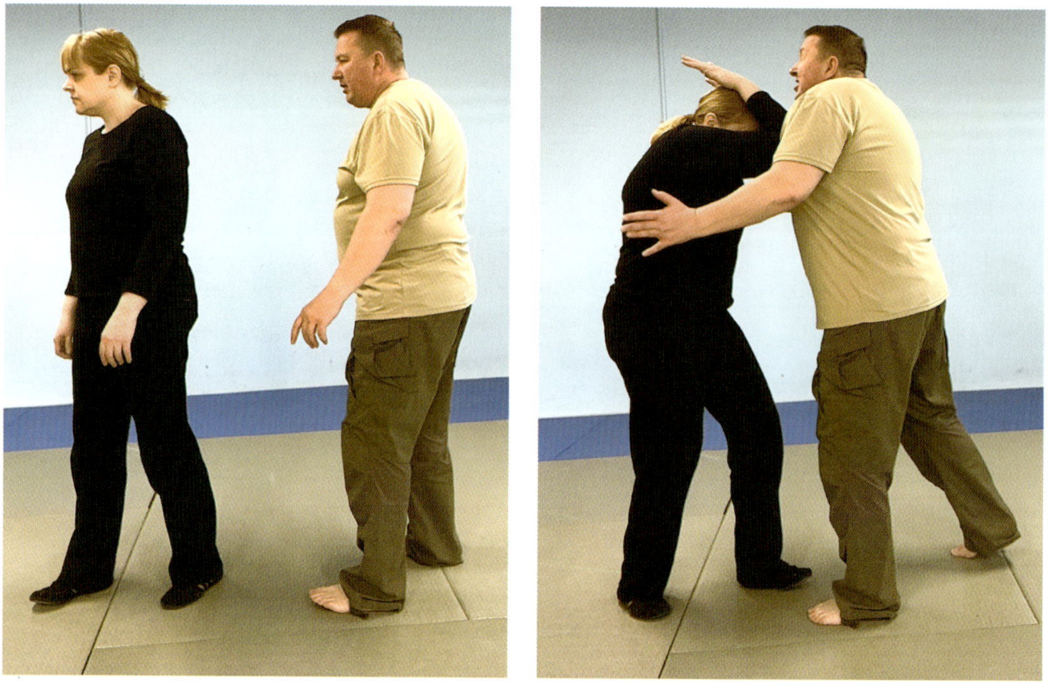

When attacked from behind the defender can turn and drive forward with double elbow punches.

The head-on defence may continue with a double hammer punch to the side of the neck and collarbones, followed by a knee kick to the groin before breaking away.

SUMMARY

Practising all these reactions from various positions provides the variability we discussed earlier. The focus of attention is placed on delivering a defensive attack at the first possible instance. The movements follow each other, and the same movement patterns can be performed by turning to the side or even when one's back is turned, requiring a 180-degree turn. Tommy Joe Moore's saying that 'Tigers don't block' is a good description of fighting. As the Finnish coat of arms bears a crowned lion with a human arm brandishing a sword, I immediately changed the tiger to a lion to describe this concept. This is also a question of intent. It is not my intention to 'block' an attacker but to stop them from continuing. Defences need to be trained so that the first strikes are to the attacker's limbs, since it may not be possible to strike to the head or torso immediately. This is an important lesson from the training methodology. It must be our intention to strike and attack all the time. This is also about the time and distance law we looked at in Chapter 3.

When asked the secret to his long life, the Finnish composer Jean Sibelius replied, 'Don't run a single step more than you need'. I have turned this into a rule: 'No movement wasted, always keep attacking'. Moving and hitting the target makes a good starting point for any physical contact practice. By using an active attacker, staying alert, following the methodology and using a lot of striking pads as targets, the training can be kept representative and safe.

In the next chapter we shall look at the basic striking techniques and the applications of strikes in different situations.

7 STRIKING WITH YOUR HANDS

Hands are our rapid response system. They are the first line of defence as well as the first line of attack. Hands are the delivery system while the power and speed come from the core and feet, or other parts of the body attached to the surface. There are multiple ways to use one's hands and in Krav Maga they are all about attacking, whether the attack is towards sensitive parts of the attacker's body, or the priority is to stop or deflect the attacker's hand or leg from hitting us, followed by our own attack to the sensitive parts of the attacker's body.

The distance and angle of the hand determines whether the punch is considered as a straight punch (jab or cross) or as a hook. The key is still the effect that the punch is there to create distraction and/or disablement. We can strike with practically any part of our hands. Once the point of contact moves towards our torso, from the elbow to the bicep/triceps area, I consider those punches more as striking with our body than with our hands.

In this chapter we will go through various basic strikes or punches using the hands. Afterwards we will learn a few exercises, illustrated by training videos that will help you to practise with a partner or even on your own.

One of the most frequently asked questions is whether it is better to hit with the fist or the palm. Frankly, hitting with open hands, using the palm, is safer since the bones of the hand are very fragile and break easily. I highly recommend to start by learning striking techniques that use open hands, and only start learning how to use your fists after the trajectories are effective. Once you start punching with fists, you should use soft targets such as balls to keep your hands healthy.

Moving on to the use of the edge of the hand, back of the hand and fingers, these are more specific. Striking with the fingers especially needs a lot of practice, but those strikes can be used to hit very precisely vulnerable parts like the throat and eyes. Let's just keep in mind that these might cause very serious damage and, while effective, they may lead to legal problems later.

PALM STRIKE

Using the palm of your hand can deliver a shocking strike to the attacker's chin, nose or collarbone and creates distance and space. It is important to get the bodyweight behind the punch and thus the kinetic chain from the palm to the ball of the feet needs to be intact.

During the movement the body balance should be slightly forward, with the feet pointing towards the opponent to maximise the ability to go forward, diagonally forward or to the side. The tension of the body is focused on the hip/waist and the core muscles. The neck area and the shoulders are more inclined to slip to the side or diagonally than behind. Tighten your core. Shoot the arm out forward. Keep your eyes on the target, as the aim is to hit the nose, jawline, collarbone area or larynx. The purpose is to create distance and effectively stop the attacker from advancing. The expected result is to see the attacker stepping back, retreating or stopped in their tracks.

It is just as important to practise hitting with the palm as with any of the punches. When practising, make sure that the way you approach the target allows you to maintain your hand's normal position. Do not attempt to employ any 90-degree angles as your wrists won't take it easily. Don't force yourself to stay in one place; it is important to move towards the target. You must put your bodyweight behind each punch and use your core to recoil the punch for the follow-up movement. A resistance band can be used to create an effective workout.

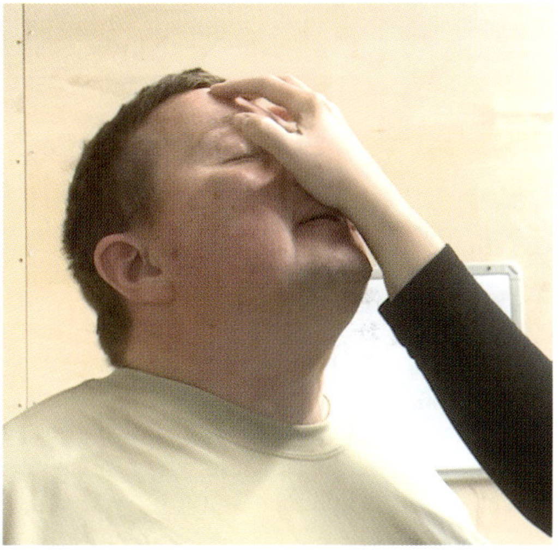

The hand position and angle of a palm strike should be natural.

Palm strike.

Clenched Fist Jab and Cross

Now, do the same exercise using your fist. The only thing that really changes from striking with an open palm is the position of your hand.

This is different from boxing, where we have gloves and hand wraps to protect our hands. The knuckles break very easily and thus it is important to understand the limitations of the fists. One of the natural biological gestures, however, is clenching the fists, so we'll need to practise hitting with them.

Striking with the bottom of the fist (hammer punch)

The hammer punch is a versatile punch that can be delivered from various body positions. The forward hammer punch is one of the most natural movements for a human being. It is the first one we attempt as infants, and it is also the commonest method of striking when holding a knife. Hammer punches go together with elbow punches since the forearm and finally the hammer will finish the job when the elbow doesn't hit, and vice versa.

The punch can be delivered with the closed fist (hammer) or with the edge of the hand (knife-hand). It can also be delivered with an open palm and fingers, making it more like a bear-claw, lion-claw or tiger-claw type of attack.

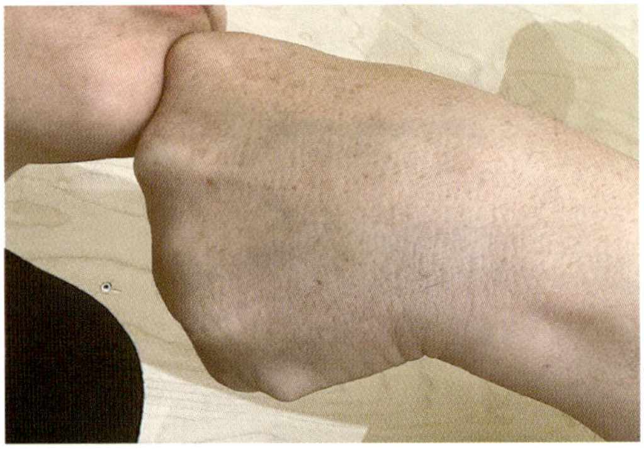

When hitting with the fist you should keep the bones aligned and ensure that the knuckle of your first finger touches the target. This will keep your hand at a good, safe angle.

Training tip

Use a Thai-boxing pad, or similar, to create the visual image of hitting the opponent's head or shoulders. You can vary the task by striking directly to the side or diagonally hitting the pad-holder's shoulder.

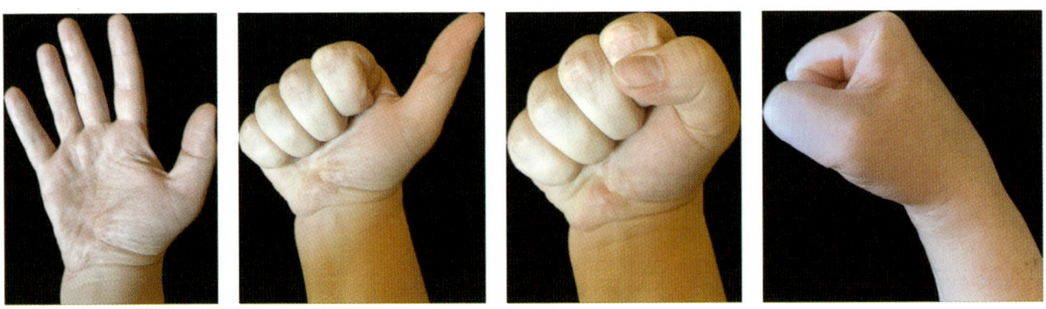

When forming a fist, start with an open palm and roll your fingers in tightly. Lock the fist with your thumb and align the knuckles with your wrist.

Striking with the back of the hand

A strike using the back of the hand is sometimes the fastest strike but there is a high risk you might break one of the most sensitive parts of your hand. The back of the hand is full of small bones that break easily, so if we hit something hard, such as the attacker's forehead, the chances are that we will break our hand. It can be a very natural movement in the right circumstances, however, and we need to learn how to use it properly.

Striking with the bottom of a clenched fist is called a hammer punch. This is a sideways hammer punch to the jawline as the continuation of an attack.

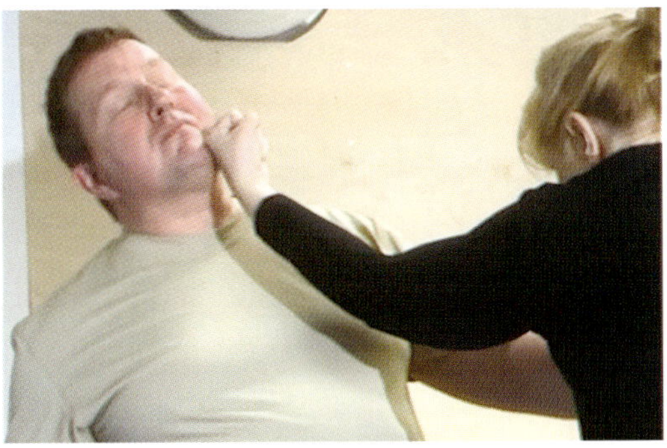

Throwing a hammer punch with the back of the hand.

To vary this hand movement, we can also use the safer means of employing the edge of the hand. What to choose depends on your action capacity and skill level. The punch is a means of driving the attacker's mind off balance and makes it possible to continue with more effective attacks.

Blade-hand strikes

Using the edge of the palm, the 'blade hand' is both a safe way to use one's hands and very effective when employed against the proper targets. This punch may be delivered in a stabbing motion or as a hammer motion. The safe target area is all around the neck except for the larynx. Hitting the larynx is deadly and you should practise so that it is deliberately avoided, which is relatively easy since we can't possibly hit the larynx area when training with a partner. It should also be noted that all full-power strikes to the neck area can cause damage and when practising these should be reserved for exercises where one can hit dummies or pads.

Hedi is using the edge of her hand to strike the side of my neck to force me off balance before continuing with a more effective attack.

> **Training tip**
>
> A blade-hand strike to the neck provides better body posture than stopping an attack by targeting the face. It is easy to practise and can be much stronger than a strike to the face. It is also morally easier to use than a direct hit to the face when applied in real-life situations.

When striking with a blade hand the target to aim for is the neck area or the back of the skull, just below the ears, in order to create distance and effectively stop the attacker from advancing. When delivered this may force the attacker to step backwards or retreat, stop them in their tracks or move their hands to cover the area hit. The attacker might also collapse, since the strike targets major blood vessels and the neural network. Any pause in bloodflow to the brain causes dizziness and even unconsciousness.

In case the strike does not have an immediate effect, there are many options by which the attack can be continued following the '+1 motion' principle.

Blade-hand strike to the sternum ('one-inch punch')

By changing the hand position from the palm to the edge of the palm, the blade hand allows us to hit targets such as the sternum and solar plexus area. The punch is very effective even from close range. The sternum doesn't hold any muscles, just the bone, and the solar plexus controls breathing. This is an easy access strike from close in when using one's hands as a fence to maintain the distance from someone behaving aggressively. It also includes the idea of Bruce Lee's 'one-inch punch', which is about timing and explosive strength. In many situations requiring force this very powerful tool is called 'distance technique'. In the starting position illustrated, Hedi's fingers are on my sternum and she is about to form a fist, but she could just as well hit through with the blade of the hand.

Starting and contact positions for the one-inch punch.

Striking with the fingers

Another way is to use your fingers to deliver the strike. In Krav Maga there is a technique called the 'educational block', which refers to using your fingers to strike the soft spot between the assailant's larynx and collarbones. Striking the eyes with the fingers is very effective and this happens automatically when targeting the nose with a palm strike.

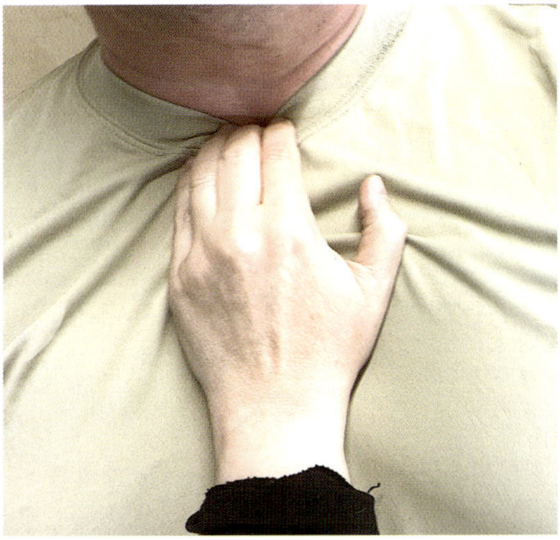

When using the educational block the fingers hit the soft part of the neck below the larynx.

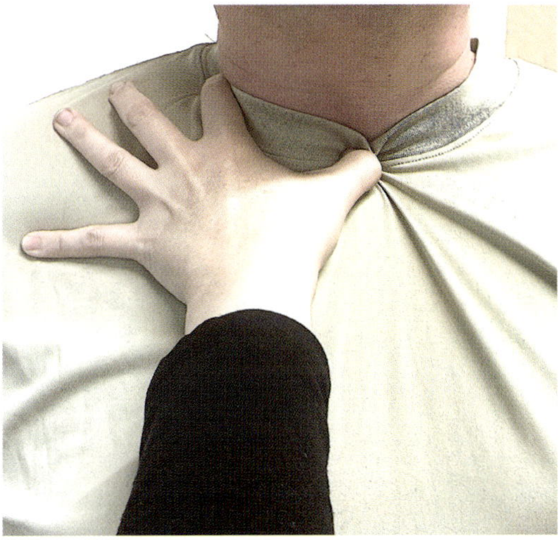

Thumb strike to the larynx.

HOOK PUNCHES

Hook punches are powerful strikes delivered either with a closed fist or an open palm. The main purpose of the hook punch is to either bypass the opponent's guard or deliver a strong attack from a closer distance than a straight punch. Let's look at a few major types and then their specific use in Krav Maga.

Hook to the groin

The groin area is a very sensitive part of the human body. Both men and women are vulnerable in this area. The direction of the strike coming from below shocks the neural points in the area, effectively passing the pain upwards from the groin. Using one's palm as a 'cup' to strike is very effective, not only in spreading the pain information but also in breaking one's balance as we instinctively protect our groin.

Hook to the groin.

Uppercut

The purpose of the uppercut is to move the opponent's head up and back at the same time. As shown here, Hedi's uppercut reaches my chin as she is using the punch to release her right hand, which I'm trying to control.

Uppercut punch.

Side hooks

Side-hook punches are delivered to targets such as the liver, solar plexus or spleen. The liver is located on the right side of the body. It is largely covered by the rib bones but its edge may be reached just under the ribcage. Punches to this area are the most likely to lead to knockouts in boxing. On the left side of the body, at about the same level as the liver, is the spleen. While a strike to the liver is more effective, any strikes under the ribcage at the sides of the body will cause the assailant to retreat.

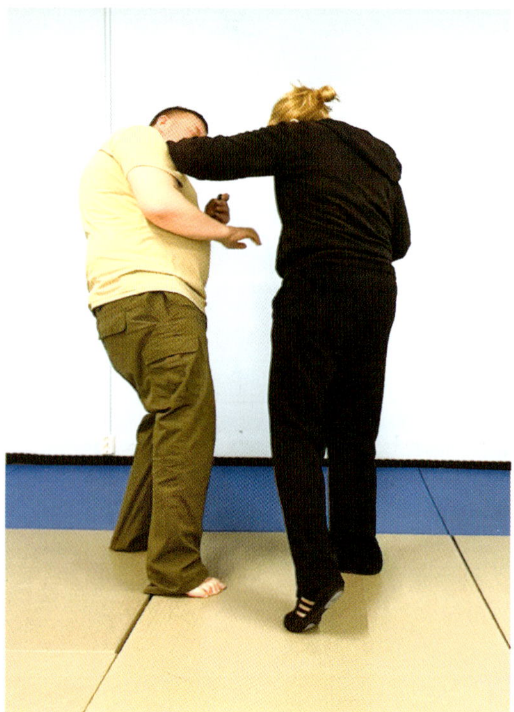

Side hooks to the body and head.

In some Krav Maga styles the principal requirement in using the hook punch is to keep the fist in the upright position. It is very much dependent on the individual's action capacity as to whether they can use their hand in such a position. As we are constantly focusing on external feedback and the targets, the hand position needs to be relevant to the task, not to the form. There are times when the hand might be turned upside down, with the thumb pointing downwards, if that might bring you closer to the outcome.

Overhand hook

The overhand hook is a mixture of a straight punch and a hook. This punch is often used in training since there are many times one needs to go over an obstacle. In boxing this reverts to a usual cross punch since it protects one's head while providing a solid attack.

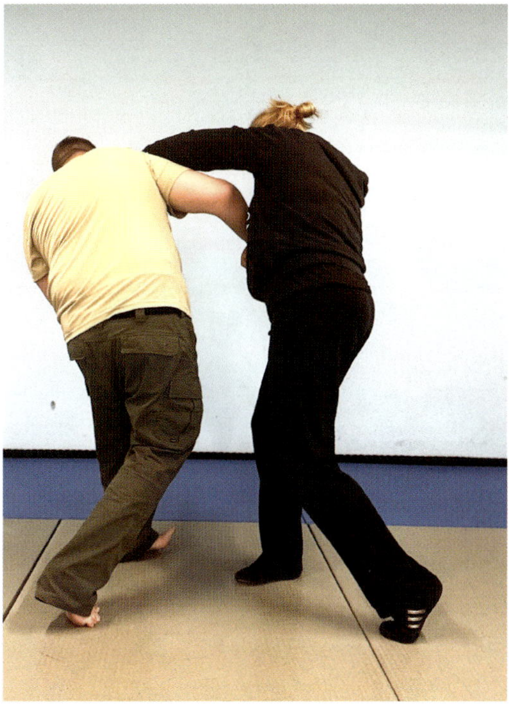

Using an overhand hook to target the opponent's jaw over his arm.

Training tip

When practising how to execute an overhand hook, the trainer should make a target with his/her left hand. The trainee takes up a fighting stance. As the trainer punches with a cross (right hand), trying to hit the trainee's right shoulder, the trainee slips and punches with an overhand hook over the trainer's hand towards the target.

ELBOW STRIKES

We will next move on to using our elbows as weapons. Elbows are extreme close-distance weapons and in Krav Maga they are also used in many defences. When combined with the one-inch punch method they are very effective at forcing the attacker off balance.

Elbows are very powerful tools that have a place in many martial arts disciplines including Thai boxing, as well as Krav Maga. To make using elbows simpler, let's focus on situations where we can't use either straight punches or hook punches. The elbow is the solution to both stopping the attacker's actions and creating space for a better solution. Seven major elbow-punch directions are employed in traditional Krav Maga:

- Elbow straight forward
- Horizontal elbow forward
- Vertical elbow forward
- Downwards straight elbow
- Elbow to the side
- Horizontal backwards
- Vertical backwards.

Elbow straight forward

This is carried out with the elbow to the front. The movement is like a jab or a cross, but performed with the elbow. This punch is intended to send the opponent directly backwards.

Elbow straight forward.

Horizontal elbow forward is like punching with a side hook, except with your elbow.

Training tip

For this exercise you will need a heavy bag as the target. Strike the bag steadily with cross punches.

Now move forward and let your forearm make contact with the bag. The bag should swing directly backwards.

The hook is often used to move the opponent off balance and allow the defender to shake themselves free.

Horizontal elbow forward

This move uses the elbow in the manner of a hook punch. It is meant to move the target sideways or diagonally backwards. It can also be applied to the back of the opponent's head if the head is already at your chest level.

Training tip

As the next stage on from the previous exercise, make contact with the heavy bag using your rear hand as you did with the cross punch. As the bag is pushed backwards, continue striking it with the elbow of your lead hand in a sideways manner. The bag should now move sideways or diagonally backwards.

Vertical elbow forward

This uses the elbow in the manner of an uppercut and is a good choice for such targets as the solar plexus, sternum and jawline. In many combat arts this is used as a means of attack. It is used in this way in Krav Maga if we need to cover our head quickly. You will see this punch being used as part of defensive moves and can also be applied to release techniques.

Training tips

Start again from the position where you have just landed a cross punch. Now move forward and hit the heavy bag with your forearm or elbow, making the bag move backwards. You can now add a side hook elbow punch to the exercise.

Downwards straight elbow

This punch is used to strike the back of the opponent's head. To be effective, the opponent needs to be in a position where his/her head is level with your waist to provide enough bodyweight behind the punch.

Training tip

Place a pad or large medicine bag on your lap or between your legs. Drive your elbows down hard onto the target.

Vertical elbow forward is like an uppercut with your elbow.

Downwards straight elbow.

Elbow to the side

This is a very good way of creating space to your side. It turns easily into a sideways (back) type of elbow strike, which should be able to do the job.

Training tips

Have your partner stand beside you holding a kick pad with his/her feet together (to provide visual feedback of when they are off balance). Hit the pad so that your partner moves backwards and then continue with a side kick or front kick, turning towards the target.

Horizontal backwards

Horizontal elbow to the rear and back. This strike is a very effective tool when performed with either an elbow or hammer-type punches. If the elbow misses the target, just let your arm extend and then swirl it back by delivering a cross punch to continue the movement.

Training tips

Have your partner hold a pad behind you. Perform three strikes (left-right-left) from a bent position. Then back up, holding the position, and repeat. You can also use a heavy bag for this.

Elbow to the side.

Horizontal elbow to the back.

VERTICAL BACKWARDS

Vertical elbow to the back. This punch is to be delivered from the position shown here. Once it has been delivered, your head needs to be lower than the target while pulling the target towards oneself. Even if the strike itself doesn't hit, it creates room for a more effective next strike, either a punch or a kick.

Training tips

Have your partner hold a pad at your head level. Lean outwards and hit the pad so that it pops upwards. Continue with a sideways hammer punch using the same hand. This develops the action capacity.

To improve your skills, go back over these exercises in slow motion with your partner very cautiously.

Vertical elbow to the back.

8 STRIKING WITH LEGS AND FEET

From knee to shin, to the balls and soles of our feet, our legs can be employed as weapons. It is also common to see people kicking with their toes – and why not, as long as one has strong pointed shoes or even steel toecaps. Let's look at the differences and how they work.

DISTANCE AND INTENTION DICTATES THE TOOL

In the pictures opposite we see examples of the different parts of the legs used in kicks. Knees, soles of the foot and the shin are for closer distances, whereas the ball of the foot can be used in a variety of distances. It is important that as we tighten our wrist area when punching, we must also tighten our ankle area when kicking. To simplify, we can separate the main striking part of the legs as follows:

- Knee strikes are especially effective close-range weapons to get the opponent off balance and break the structure. In Krav Maga knee kicks are integrated into almost every defensive action.
- The sole of the foot, together with the edge of the sole when we're barefoot, provides a good stomping tool.
- The heel of the foot is effective when we need to kick at a backwards angle.
- The shin is an excellent tool for both defensive and offensive striking.
- The ball of the foot provides an effective way of striking precisely at such targets as the groin, the solar-plexus or even the jaw.

A knee kick is an effective close-range weapon.

The heel is an effective way to hit targets behind you.

The sole of the foot can be used in a stamping forward kick.

The shin can be used defensively against a kick.

The ball of the foot can be employed as part of a defensive forward kick.

KNEE KICKS

The knees are often used to target the groin/hip area. They are also extremely effective weapons when targeted to the sides and back of the thighs, helping to force the person off balance and give you the advantage when making other attacks. The kneecap itself doesn't work well when hitting hard surfaces, so aim for softer targets such as muscles or the groin. Hitting someone to the head with a knee kick is extremely effective, but again it needs to be justified from the legal point of view. Don't set yourself up to end every situation with a knee kick to the face, but limit its use in training to representative targets. You must also avoid full-speed knee kicks to the head in training, as our necks can't take that.

Action capacity training tips

Use a heavy bag or have your training partner hold a pad beside him/her (not on him/her, because you won't see the effects). Hold on to your training partner or the heavy bag and deliver a knee kick, followed immediately by an elbow. Repeat the exercise.

Stomping kick forward

The stomping kick forward is used both for attack and for defence. In Krav Maga we are taught to stomp on the opponent's instep, but as this is such a fragile place, we very rarely get to practise the move. As we can't practise it on the target, it ought to be hard to use, but fortunately the construction industry supplies types of safety boots that offer a possibility to practise the move. If I use my front leg to perform a stomping kick in this situation, that turns into something like a side kick, only with less bodyweight behind it. A side kick, or back kick with the instep at a horizontal angle, is the reverse motion to the stomping kick forward.

Training tips

Exercise 1: Stomping kick forward

- Place a target, such as a kick pad, at an angle of 45 degrees.
- Raise your leg up as in the picture on the previous page demonstrating how to use the sole of the foot.
- Strike your leg downwards into the pad, recoil and move to a punch.

Exercise 2: Forwards and backwards

- Stomp kick forward, recoil and then stomp your kick backwards with the same leg.
- If you wish, wrap a rubber band around the sole of your foot and let that give you resistance to the kick. This makes a good balance and core exercise.

FRONT KICKS

Two main front kicks are used in Krav Maga. One I refer to as 'come closer to me', since when hit to the groin it will make the opponent bend forward from the hip, bringing his jawline closer for me to punch.

The other one I call 'get away from me', as it sends the opponent backwards. This is also known as a pushing front kick. When used in this sense, you must hit the target and put your bodyweight behind the kick so that it lands strongly forward. It is very challenging to maintain your balance, however, because if you miss the target all the bodyweight is behind the kick, sending you easily off balance.

Attacking or lifting front kick

This kick is usually performed by hitting with the ball of the foot, penetrating the groin area deeply. It is very common, however, to see this performed with the instep of the foot. Done this way it lacks the full potential that comes from the knee being higher than the impact zone. The knee joint acts as the hinge, and the power will be transferred all the way until the leg is straight. When hitting with the instep the knee straightens before the impact. This way does not affect the structure or the balance, but relies solely on the pain it causes. That is not the strategy to choose.

The lifting front kick is about drawing the opponent closer to punch them.

The defensive front kick is intended to drive the opponent away or stop them in their tracks.

Defensive or pushing front kick

When the defensive front kick is employed the knee comes first and then the hip sends the kick on its way in a direct push or hit. Here Hedi is shown performing the kick with the front leg, but both legs can naturally be used to deliver the kick. It all depends on the distance. Every kick must be accompanied by a consecutive attack, whether another kick or punch, or taking the opportunity to leave the scene.

Action capacity training tips

The older we get, the harder it gets to move our hips in the optimal way. Here are two exercises to help maintain your action capacity or even improve it.

Exercise 1

- Start lifting your knee up to the front and the side.
- Once you lift the knee to the side, bring it forward like a roundhouse knee kick.
- Now start extending your leg forward as you kick the knee in.
- You have also just learned how to mask your front kick.

Exercise 2

- Now that your hip has been warmed up, it's time to move to front kicks.
- Place a knee-high obstacle in front of your kicking leg, such as a heavy bag lying sideways.
- Now lift your leg and kick, preferably against a target, to see the result.

When using the defensive front kick always make sure the knee is higher than the striking spot.

BACK KICKS

Just as front kicks have two main purposes, so do the back kicks. An attacking back kick moves from down to up, while a defensive back kick shoots straight backwards. The distinction between a back kick and side kick is the direction of the foot: with the back kick the toes point downwards, while with the side kick they point diagonally downwards. This is not really relevant when our intention is simply to repeat the outcome, but it is something that we should know for the sake of general knowledge.

A feature that distinguishes Krav Maga from many martial arts is the way the kicks are practised. As the back kick is needed to deal with threats behind us, that is where the training starts.

Action capacity training tips

- Have a training partner hold the kick pad while standing beside it to avoid any knee injuries and provide visual feedback of your kick.
- Start by making a defensive kick followed by an attacking kick, advancing as you do so (your partner will be moving backwards while you're doing this).
- This way you will learn how to step in and use the advancement methodology at the same time.
- If you want to emphasise keeping your body position low, have your training partner swing a (soft) stick at your normal head level. This environmental constraint will remind you to stay down.

A defensive back kick pushes an opponent off balance by forcing their hips backwards.

SIDE KICK

The side kick is a very powerful tool to send someone backwards. It couples your body defence against a punch or even a stabbing move towards your neck, and stops the attacker in their tracks.

In this exercise Hedi has started to punch towards my face. As I moved away from the punch and used my hand to defend myself, I loaded the leg up to be sent her way. As I extend my leg, my hip also opens, shifting the toes of my base leg so they are directed in the opposite direction.

I can then either let my kicking leg land close to Hedi and then continue with the hammer punch cross-front kick combination or turn to take a few fast steps and position myself where I can better assess the situation.

This exercise is all about the combat mindset, your OODA loop and, finally, your body balance.

The side kick is an effective way of stopping an opponent from launching an attack and then preventing them from running after us.

Action capacity training tips

- As with the back kick exercise, have a training partner hold a kick pad for you.
- Make sure that the training partner stays just behind your waistline.
- Make sure that the toes of your kicking leg are pointing down diagonally. If they are not you should just resort to a front kick.

ROUNDHOUSE KICKS

In Krav Maga the first roundhouse kick is one that comes up at an angle of 45 degrees. It is well suited for occasions when you might dodge to the side and deliver a front kick. As your body is tilted to the side and your leg will be sideways, this makes it in effect a roundhouse kick. Another way this happens is where you let the roundhouse kick drive through as a secondary attack to a cross punch. In this attack the kick might well be a low roundhouse kick of the type often seen in combat sports. A roundhouse kick might also be delivered with the knee, shin or the ball of the foot. As with the attacking front kick, the knee should pass the impact point.

Low roundhouse kick

The purpose of the roundhouse kick is to pass the opponent's guard and break their balance. This is the most important function in self-defence. Whereas in combat sports the roundhouse kick might be the end of a combination, in self-defence something always needs to happen after it, if only increasing the distance between you and your attacker.

Action capacity training tips

Exercise 1

- This exercise requires a long, heavy bag.
- Start by placing your shin on the bag so that your knee comes out from one side and your ankle/instep from the other.
- Give a 'one-inch punch' with your hip and recoil.
- Repeat and maintain your balance.

Exercise 2

- Have your training partner stand behind the heavy bag and throw you a cross punch with a soft stick or similar (to represent the reach).
- Slip and deliver a low roundhouse kick.
- Continue with punches or attacks using the knee.

Roundhouse kick against an advancing opponent

The roundhouse kick for use against an advancing opponent is the first we encounter in training as it is relatively easy to turn a front kick into a roundhouse kick just by moving one's upper body to the side, away from a punch or similar attack.

The action capacity training exercises described earlier can be turned into skill training by adding aspects of perception-action coupling. In order to make a distinction between a front kick and a roundhouse, for example, place an obstacle as an environmental constraint between attacker and defender.

Reverse roundhouse kick

The reverse roundhouse kick makes it possible to attack targets that are behind us and cannot be hit either with punches (too far away) or with back kicks (too close).

The situation illustrated is a moment in time when Hedi perceives an opportunity to strike me to the groin with a reverse roundhouse kick by passing my front leg. As the strike comes in, my hip will be moving backwards. This gives Hedi an opportunity to turn towards me and continue with a combination of hammer punch, cross and front kick/roundhouse kick, so creating the distance to disappear.

Roundhouse kick horizontal forward. The idea is to kick above the obstacle and strike the opponent.

Reverse roundhouse kick.

Action capacity training tips

As it is important to have the capacity to kick from a bent position, we can use a wall to help us maintain balance.

- Lean against a wall with the shoulder of your base leg side.
- Turn your head so that you can see the target.
- Deliver an attacking (lifting) back kick to a focus pad.
- Now place a kick pad between you and the target and kick over it (you can alter the height as necessary).
- By adding perception-action coupling the exercise is turned into a skill.

SUMMARY

Training for kicks is fun! There is so much more to practising kicking high and low than just their self-defence applications. Kicks provide the tools to get your core aligned with them (and also with punches), making your body work like a well-oiled machine. Using the kicks as sweeps to target your opponent's ankles is an application that can be picked up quickly. Sweeps are not the solution we are looking for in Krav Maga, but like joint locks they are something that come up in the course of training.

These links to YouTube videos will help you explore ideas for training:

'Black Belt Date Night'

https://youtu.be/ZrSgLlWC-3g?si=LqZru82hFbeGIQL9

'10x your learning with task simplification'

https://youtu.be/yWAZEar8fnw?si=7B0OVKldekGApqBa

9 DEFENSIVE STRIKING

The idea that 'Lions don't block', introduced earlier, is the reason why I don't use the word 'block' when referring to stopping an attacker's incoming limb. Krav Maga is very much like catch wrestling in that there are no defences, just attacks. Training becomes easier once we overcome the idea of seeking a perfect block to stop the attacker's intentions. However, just as with attacking striking, which means hitting what breaks and hurts, we'll need to do some action capacity training.

Action capacity in defensive striking is needed to make these subconscious movements conscious. By understanding how, and why, our hands and legs move from various body positions, the training of defensive striking becomes easier. Blocking is never the intention, but it is a way of making it possible to do what is necessary to stop the attacker's intentions. The same idea will arise when we move on to release techniques.

DEFLECTION, POWER REVERSAL (STOPPING), SLIDING

It is helpful to understand how the main characteristics of defensive striking fit into the bigger picture. Deflection means that by striking the incoming limb we alter its direction. Power reversal, or stopping, means that the incoming limb is struck in a straightforward line, sending it back in the direction it was coming from. Sliding is similar to deflection, but the limb is not affected in a manner that causes it to change direction. Defence and defensive striking is there to enable us to reach the destination of stopping the attacker's intentions.

When practising defensive action, it is important to design the practice so that the defence is needed and there are no other options available. A practical methodology for this is to start the exercise so that the defence-player has his/her back towards the attack-player, and after turning round they have to face whatever incoming attack is required by the goal of the exercise.

Another method is to train at such proximity that the only option available is defensive striking. Altering the stances will then create constraints that naturally lead to certain defences in the way they were intended. The task is still to attack and integrate defensive striking into the action. It is an effective form of training that will help us judge the success-failure rate (*see* Chapter 4).

HEAD LEVEL DEFENCES

All defences are the result of perception-action coupling. To make better sense I have divided them by the height and the direction of the defender's movement. In each case I will describe the mental and physical starting positions from which the specific defensive striking methods will emerge.

Inside defence within slip and cross

In Chapter 1 we introduced the idea of 'move and fire'. Now let's bring the attack-player a little closer. The two actions should be as simultaneous as possible, with the attack leading the defence. The reaction we're looking for is to bring the head diagonally forward. The defender's task is to hit the attacker's ribcage/liver. Again, you should use striking pads to make it possible to strike with full power.

The defender starts from an inside defence stance with their head down a little. The attack-player starts side-on to the defender and then tries to hit with a cross to the defender's chest (make sure this is protected), before continuing with a lead hook (open palm) to his/her ribs.

Training tips

One idea is to hold a soft ball in your striking hand, place your defending hand in position and then try to hit the defender in the face. Hold the end position and see what needs to be achieved before moving on.

Inside defence with the front hand

Building on the move and fire analogy, the jab turns into a defensive strike that continues with a cross. This defence is built on the natural human instinct to push the danger away with one's hand. To train the motion, start from the middle of the movement as shown overleaf. To bring about the natural head movement, use attacks such as an uppercut punch with the cross hand and continue with a lead side hook to the head. The defender's aim is to force the attacker off balance. This is done by leaning forward and continuing with a cross punch, sending the attack-player diagonally backwards. Make sure you use pads or balls to enable the powerful strikes essential to get the feedback needed to decide on how to continue.

Training tips

The attacker needs to startle the defender, perhaps by starting the punch unexpectedly. The direction of the defender's reaction will reveal whether this technique can be completed or the defender should solve it with some other movement.

Sometimes starting the attack with an uppercut is a more helpful way of assessing the defender's reaction.

Inside defence. The front hand is in the starting position. The body will follow as the hand shoots forward.

Inside defence. The front hand has completed its travel, ready for the second line of attacks.

Shielding the head

This technique hasn't been included in traditional Krav Maga, but it is described here as it is the initial movement for the Krav Maga 360 defence at the head level. This defence is a very common technique in many combat sports and martial arts. The difference in Krav Maga is how it is taught by coupling it to an active situation, such as part of a release that will be described in Chapter 11.

This movement solution was also present earlier when we looked at the startle-flinch response as the attacker was trying to wrap his hands around the defender in a bear hug. This brought the attacker close enough for a line of defence to emerge. For this to work the defender should have his/her hands up, although a regular defence stance or an inside defence stance also work well. The continuation of the defence offered two main options, either continuing with an elbow punch to the chin or a double hammer punch to the side of the neck or collarbones. Both movements make it possible to follow up with a kick.

Stabbing defence (head level)

A forward stabbing defence is what might be called a 'general solution'. Its origin comes from an attack in which both hands shoot out to grab the attacker by the head or, in a military context, his helmet. The best way to train for this defence is to start in the fighting stance with hands open. It is also possible to adopt a sideways position so that the defender turns inwards towards the attacker.

This movement is trained in many Krav Maga styles as the defence against a stick or bat attack coming from above. Its importance, however, comes more from its place in decision-making whether to move out first or stay close in.

In closed spaces, where the impact sends the attacker backwards but the movement may be stopped by a wall, the next movement is to grab the back of the neck with a scooping motion and hit the groin area with the knee, landing the attacker at the defender's feet.

Stabbing defence against a threat coming from above.

360 defence at had level.

360 defence (head level)

The 360 defence is a reflex that emerges when a fast-moving object is coming towards our body. Coupling this with a simultaneous attack, however, is very controversial as the movement is traditionally practised from a neutral stance with hands down (*see* Chapter 4). If we want the defence and attack to be simultaneous, we must start and focus on the attack, then allow the defence to emerge. After all, 'Lions don't block'. On the other hand, once our head has moved away from the danger, we can learn to couple it with a kick and then move in any direction that best helps us to deal with the situation.

Training tips

Start with the defender punching jabs and crosses to a single pad held by the attacker, who throws circular punches either with his/her hand or the pad. The striking continues regardless of the defences. The attacker moves according to the punches, which is usually backwards. This helps to keep the distance and body balance intact.

Front hand defending against the front hand

If our leading hand prevents the attacker's front hand from grabbing us, for example, an immediate second attack is required. In the case shown here Hedi is using her defensive hand to deliver a backhand strike towards my chin, followed by a strong cross punch. Should the attacker try to punch with a cross, this might lead to an outside defence or stabbing defence, coupled with either a punch or a kick. The choice is dictated by the head movement.

Training tips

The attacker should vary their intentions, while the defender should vary their starting posture.

Varying the height of the attack will lead to other defensive actions becoming apparent.

Front hand defending against front hand defensive strike.

Continuing the attack from front hand defending against front hand. Taken a fraction of a second after the blow connected, note how the cross hand is already preparing to go for the jawline.

Two-handed defence

Imi Lichtenfeld claimed that one of the key lessons he learned from street fighting was never to commit to any attack with both hands. That is a worthy goal, but sometimes psychology decides differently. The reflex to push danger away with both hands together is the founding principle of stabbing defence, in which our body provides the attack alongside the inner forearm to the neck.

It is very instinctive to use a two-handed defence against, for example, a high roundhouse kick or some type of attack with a baton or stick. This involves similar problems, and the ways of solving them, to those we encountered with the previous technique where the front hand is defending against the opponent's front hand.

While delivering the defensive strikes, put the emphasis on how the closer hand should be striking the knee area. (This would be the elbow area when training against a stick or bat.) Move while delivering a backhand strike to the attacker's chin and complete the sequence with a cross. Naturally there will be the option to continue with a front kick as the attacker moves backwards.

The two-handed defence at head level is the immediate response to a roundhouse kick towards the head.

Training tips

Start the exercise from the side position. Always use pads so you can employ forceful or even full-impact strikes. Use a kick pad as the target to give proper feedback as to the full force behind the attack.

Training tips

The defender should start with their hands in the defensive action posture. The attacker then punches with a cross hand upper and lead-hand side hook attack. The defender must then take the attacker off balance with a lead-hand defensive strike. The focus of attention in the attack should be the need to take the attacker off balance.

Double defence: one hand up, one hand down

The double defence is a result of body movement in which the left foot stays in front. Should the movement instead take the left foot backwards, the defence turns into a shoulder-defence type of action. The lead hand has most contact with the attacker's hand, taking him/her off balance while the cross hand will be used to attack.

This defence is often seen when defending against a slashing motion with a blade. When done correctly, the defender moves forward diagonally during the defence. This works if the attacker is truly committed to the attack, but if he/she is not, there is a huge problem as the attacker gives up instantly when contact is made. This then leads the defender to head straight towards the attacker and perhaps result in the defender being slashed and stabbed. This is always a possibility, but in that case the defence needs to be changed.

Double defence, with the front hand facing upwards and the rear hand downwards.

MIDSECTION DEFENSIVE ACTION

The midsection extends from our elbows to the groin. Depending on the angle of attack and the stance (hand position) adopted, several possible defences may become apparent.

Inside Forearm Defence

This hand defence method provides forearm defence against grabbing, stabbing or strikes to targets such as the solar plexus, liver, spleen and stomach. It starts with an inside defence stance with the lead hand responding. The intention is to strike with the rear hand (cross) while the lead hand is deflecting the attacker's arm towards his other hand. In the exercise illustrated Hedi commences the hand defence once I start pushing my hand forward and pulling it back, trying to throw another punch with the other hand.

Starting position for the inside forearm defence. Here the attacker is reaching forward to grab the defender's wrist.

The defender responds by throwing the forearm forward, while already preparing the cross hand to strike the attacker's jaw.

Finishing position of the inside forearm defence. Note that this and the previous photo are two stages of the same movement, not separate steps.

Elbow-forearm defence

Start from a bladed position with the lead hand down. Hedi's intention here is to strike me on my stomach or try to grab something from my belt. As I make the defence, I'm simultaneously moving diagonally forward and flipping my defending hand over her hand to take her off balance.

The elbow forearm defence comes into play when the attacker's hand is coming over the defender's front hand.

The elbow-forearm defence brings the defender moving forward diagonally, pushing the attacker off balance, followed by punches to the neck or face.

Training tips

Start again from the point where the defence makes contact. The attacker starts to push her hand forward and then pull it back while hitting with the other hand. The attacker can then raise her attacking lead hand to play the part of her head for the defender to strike.

Shoulder burst defence

The shoulder burst defence is an elbow-high forearm defence from closer in. This defence is presented in many Krav Maga sequences as a solution to adopt against a baseball bat or a high roundhouse kick. It might come up when faced with these attacks, but the defender should then be walking towards the attacker with the inside defence stance to guard against low attacks (lead hand down).

360 Defence Midsection

This defence response emerges from various situations, such as when the forearm defence has been more sliding and not deflected the attacker's actions, the attacker has not been taken off balance and so his hand has recoiled to the starting position. The defence starts by striking the side of the neck while pushing forward with the hands arranged in a sort of letter 'A'. The defender should take hold of the attacker's hand as it passes the attacker's waist. This eventually forces the attacker's bodyweight to move backwards. If his head remains high, he will fall on his back even without the help of a sweeping back kick. Should the attacker's chin drop to his chest, the defender needs to move to his side and either bring him down from there or use other attacks. This is where a variety of different responses might occur. Depending on the state of the combat mindset (white, yellow, orange, red), and thus the stance, we can expect numerous different 'move and fire' solutions.

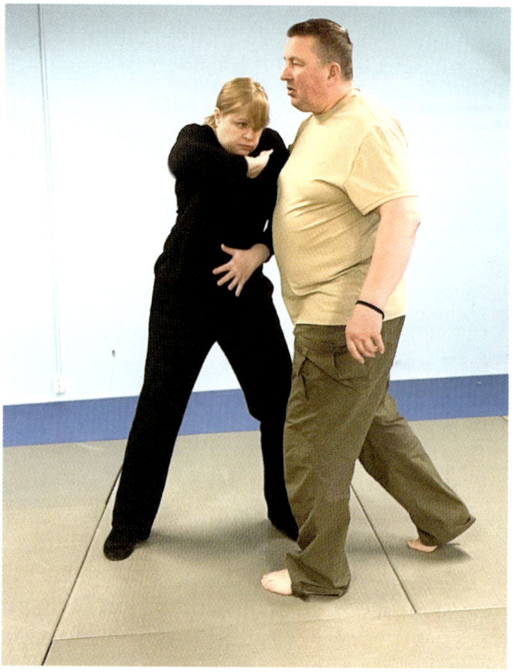

Shoulder burst defence response. Something startles the defender from the side, making her shoulder rise to protect the head and bring up the opposite hand to cover the face.

Following the shoulder burst defence response, the defender can hit the attacker's chest with her shoulder and follow through with a forward elbow punch to send the attacker back.

When using the 360 forearm torso-level defence the defender counters with a forearm to the neck, sending the attacker backwards.

The defender then follows the attacker and, when his hand passes his waistline, takes an underhook hold of the arm and continues bursting forward.

The defender may finish off the attack by hitting the attacker's neck so that his head moves backwards behind his heel line, causing him to fall.

DEFENCES AGAINST KICKS TO THE GROIN

Even though Krav Maga is well known for its use of kicks to the groin, football players are just as adept at this 'sport'. The kicking movement is so natural that even a toddler does it without being taught anything about kicking. Give one a ball to keep their hands busy and the kicks will soon follow. That football-kicking motion is very common on real-life videos of violent encounters involving kicks. There are, in addition, trained solutions such as the front kick and even the roundhouse kicks.

It is important to learn how to defend against attacks of this type, especially when we're not responding quickly enough to just move and fire. The defensive hand defence motions include sliding and deflecting strikes. Legs can also be used to stop attacks or strike in response.

The stabbing kick defence is based on the move and fire solution, moving forward diagonally and delivering a jab. The attacker here delivers a kick to the groin that needs to be dealt with. The focus should be on attacking, not blocking.

Stabbing defence against a strike to the groin

The basis of this defence is a forward diagonal movement coupled with a lead hand jab. At the same time the opponent replies with a kick to the groin, forcing the defender's rear hand to make a stabbing motion to avoid getting hit. The attack should lead, not the defence. Should the defence lead, the body will revert to moving to the side, changing the first attack into a side kick.

Training tips against kicks will be found in the YouTube video 'Stabbing defense down 2024: Train this way and get fast results' (https://youtu.be/xITQe99p_TA).

Scooping defence against a kick. The reflex sends the hand downwards in a 360-type of motion, but as the palm is facing downwards it is more natural to scoop the leg outwards, deflecting the kick, than let it slide. The front hand is moving so it can attack with a punch to the sternum or face, or just push the attacker off balance using an inside hand defence.

Scooping defence against a strike to the groin

The origin of the scooping hand-defence is a forearm defence down, known as a 360 in Krav Maga. As we perceive the strength of the attack, the kick can be deflected in a

Training tips

- Imagine a scenario involving a fight with an attacker carrying an oriental knife and start from the first point of contact.
- The attacker starts by shoving the knife towards the defender's stomach.
- The defender scoops the knife and wraps his/her hands around the attacker's hand, striking his/her shoulder against the back of the attacker's shoulder to force them off balance, and then making an escape.
- You can vary this by scooping and then deflecting the attacker's hand to upset their balance, before continuing with a punching solution and escaping.
- Repeat the exercise, but this time with kicking. Make sure both participants are wearing shin protectors.
- You can also use a kick pad to simulate the striking power.

Once the leg has been deflected, the hand has made connect with the attacker and the defender has moved forward diagonally, it is time to take the initiative and attack.

scooping motion. In the event that we have been startled and the lead hand is not ready to lead the movement, the defence might be followed with a front kick or a stomping kick to the attacker's base leg. The intention is to take the attacker off balance as soon as possible.

Inside palm defence against a strike to the groin

From my experience, this defence has every risk of breaking your fingers if you attempt to force it from a body posture that doesn't support the natural movement. The natural response to something coming towards

If we face a sudden kick attack to the groin when we are resting in a non-violent position, the body will move away immediately, taking the hand with it.

Training tips

- Start from the point of contact at the waist level. Vary the combat mindset you are aiming for by trying different tasks such as counting, talking and reading.
- Arrange for someone to startle you by delivering a fast incoming movement using a soft stick or similar that will not cause any damage.
- Go towards the source of the movements and use constraints to help you assess the solution.

one's groin is to push the danger away, so that motion is better suited to a scooping defence. A palm defence, however, can be a very natural movement provided it is done from a starting point that supports it. The way of continuing the movement after contact is very much the same as before.

Start from the inside defence stance intended for low strikes, holding the lead hand down as though you were calming someone down. The attacker then kicks with his/her lead leg towards the defender's groin. This defence may also be performed from a closer range using a rear-leg knee kick instead of a front kick.

Forearm defence against a strike to the groin

This defence is a natural movement for anyone holding something in their lead hand or if their fist is clenched. It is like the defence against a stab, grab or punch targeting the stomach described earlier. Experience has shown that it is a very natural movement against a roundhouse kick to the groin, provided you start from the stance where your lead hand is level with your waist.

The defence can be trained for alongside that for the elbow-forearm defence described earlier.

DEFENDING KICKS WITH KICKS

There is much truth in the saying that an attack is the real defence. This is especially true when we're faced with defending low kicks or have early warning of a kick attack coming in.

Stomping kick defence

A sequence that includes a stomping kick against the attacker trying to kick us and then following up with hand strikes is a very Krav Maga approach. The problem is that training this at full speed is very likely to result in injuries. One solution is to start by making it an attack and then adding the movement that would be instigated by the attacker.

Training tips

- Use kick pads to simulate the attack as this could well be done against someone swinging down onto you a blunt object such as a skateboard.
- Moving from defensive to attacking action is key to the training, so be careful to use heavy bags or similar objects to enable you to strike at full power.
- This is one of the main attacking methods used in military zero-distance encounters when a weapon has malfunctioned and we need another way of countering the enemy. I can confirm it works great under pressure.

Inside defence with the shin

This is a fast-response movement to protect the groin against strikes coming from below. Its origin is the natural movement by which we retract our groin and hip, with the knee turning inside naturally. It is easy to train with a stick at close range to get the action right, though you should ensure you are wearing shin and groin protection.

Inside defence with the shin.

Outside defence with the shin

This defence is very familiar from Thai boxing, where it is very much part of the game, as well as in K1 kickboxing and other kicking combat arts. In Krav Maga this defence arises in situations where the attacker is trying to throw a lead hand jab and the defender is slipping and kicking a roundhouse to the attacker's groin, forcing the need for the shin defence or risk getting hit.

Outside defence with the shin.

SUMMARY

Starting to learn Krav Maga is about putting the emphasis on attacking. Learning how to hit effectively then leads us to use defensive striking between attacks. The constraints-led approach is a very good method in learning to strike defensively and we must create situations where the movements emerge naturally. It is important to keep the attacks at the same speed they appear in real life. Keeping the tasks simple and applying non-linear teaching methods will help in acquiring skills. Slowing down the attacks gives the wrong information and that doesn't support learning. We will next move on to situations where the attacker has succeeded in getting hold of us. While learning how to deal with these issues, we will again need to rely on representative practice design and a non-linear approach to learning.

10 RELEASES FROM GRABS AND HOLDS

The area of self-defence that covers releases from various grabs, holds and chokes is both the easiest and the hardest to learn: the easiest since we can easily make it come alive and scale the resistance with the skill level, and the hardest because we may start to think of it as pure mechanics and forget about the emotions and psychology. Let's start from the first point of contact, which is usually the hands.

When training to defend against grabs and holds, it is also important to learn how to attack with them. That's why the training starts with learning how to attack and what the attacker's intentions might be. This is how we learn to take in correct information. Adding a bit of yelling at some time helps to enhance the natural body positions and the startle-flinch response.

HAND RELEASES

The hand releases are a combination of mechanics and the use of one's core. It is mechanics in a sense that we'll force the opponent's hand to an angle that forms a joint-lock and, while doing so, use our core muscles to release. It is important to understand that we'll need to bring our elbows close to our body, or move our body close to the elbows. In Krav Maga we approach all these releases from the striking point of view.

One of the hardest things to learn to do instinctively is changing the natural response of trying to pull away into one of closing in. On the other hand, learning to change direction quickly when stuck is no problem. It is also important to remember that it is acceptable to hurt and even injure a person who is

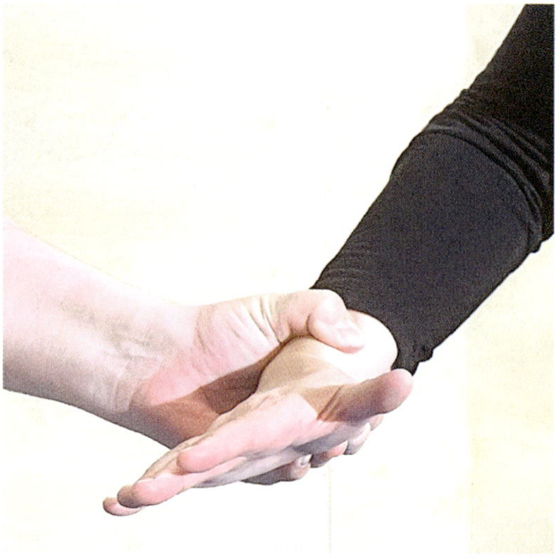

Wrist hold using the gap between thumb and forefinger gap to restrict the opponent's use of their hand.

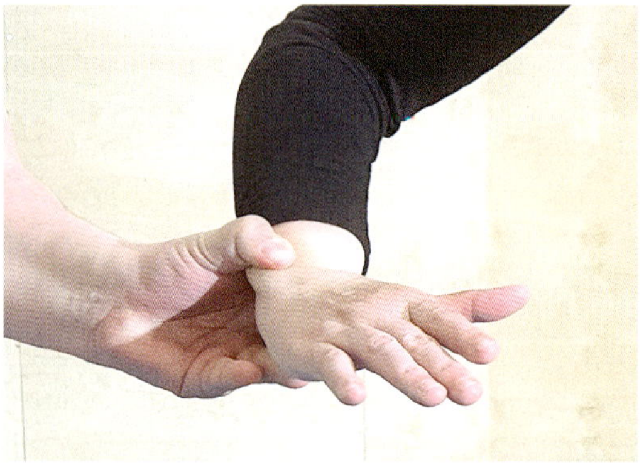

Keep pushing the elbow forward while your forearm stays horizontal.

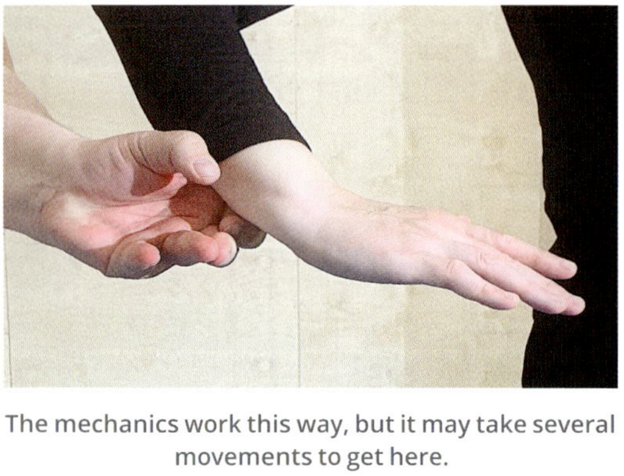

The mechanics work this way, but it may take several movements to get here.

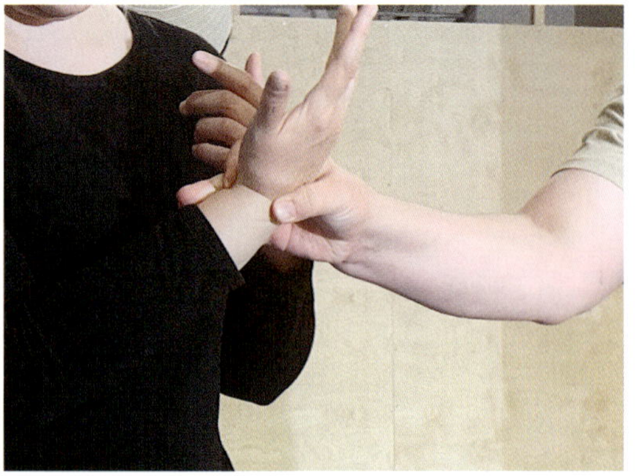

Releasing with the assisting defensive striking is a soft option that will make it hard for the attacker to continue.

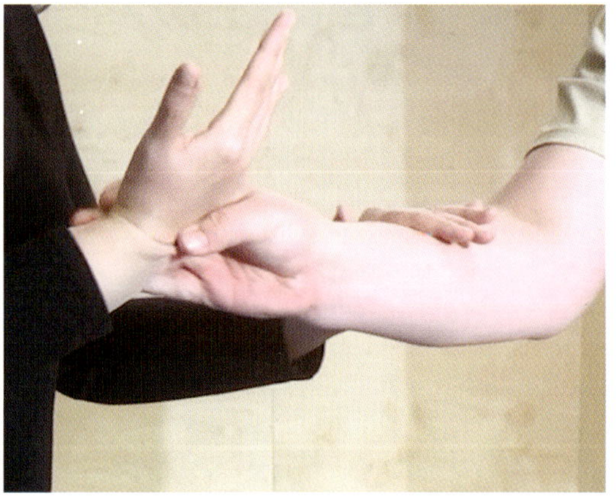

Use your free hand to do the defensive inside defence!

Training tips

Start the catching hands game from the situation where one of you has a solid grip on the other's hand. Now release and immediately grip the other's hand. Repeat the exercise changing the angles and heights.

grabbing you. It is all about the context, since what might happen next after he gets hold of you is what we are stopping.

Strike with your front hand and at the same release the hand backwards. Be ready to move away or continue attacking.

From the front

Think of a situation where a person is harassing you and trying to hold your hand, but you can't get away. Let's go back to the first lesson on punching. Arrange your body so that your rear leg is on the side from which you are being grabbed, which makes hip movement easier. Now bring your lead hand in between, with the elbow downwards to stop the attacker easily passing your hand, and take you in something like a rear-naked choke hold. As you release your hand you will now be able to create more distance. If talking doesn't work, punch either to the side of the neck or with your fingers to the throat, bringing your weight forward and sharply pivoting your hip.

From the front, both hands locked high

Think of a situation where we have started to calm the person down, but he/she is not having any of it and instead grabs our hands and starts pushing us back. A way of making

When both of your arms are held at the front, start the release by attacking with elbow punches and continue with more forward elbow punches.

them release their grip is to use elbow striking. The trick is to punch one's elbow forward and above the attacker's elbow while moving diagonally forward, then repeating the movement with the other hand.

From the side

When someone grabs you by the arm, that is not the actual attack, which might be when they then drag you somewhere. The response is to balance oneself and, while doing so, use

Release your arm by forming an elbow punch, pulling it in sharply and then punching towards the assailant. Depending on how you assess the threat, you can continue with a hammer punch.

When being pulled towards an attacker, our immediate response is to try to pull back. This becomes the starting point for the 'anchor, balance, attack' response.

Once you have balanced yourself, turn your elbow down and use a defensive forearm strike to push the assailant off balance.

the hand being held for a defensive strike such as a Krav Maga 360-type of defence and then continue as needed. The natural response is to pull the arm away and we want to enhance that. If you are pulled towards the attacker, however, your body will move differently. That's why two set of responses need to be learned. When the attacker makes a definite move, for example driving you against a wall and grabbing you, it isn't necessary to remember any movements, just release yourself by using defensive striking.

From behind

It might be hard to imagine this situation ever happening. If your hands are down, for example, what would be the reason to grab him/her by the wrists? It could happen, though, if you are standing and someone seated wants to pull you onto his lap. If both of you are on your feet, the probability is that the hold will be around your bicep-elbow area. In both cases a good starting point is to use the startle-flinch response to your advantage while striking the opponent with your hip and then immediately using elbow strikes.

The biggest mistake we can make when learning the hand releases is to focus on the mechanics while disregarding the psychological side of our body functions. The sight of the defender holding their arm straight out in front while the attacker just stands there immobile, is something that needs to end. The key is making the training dynamic, pacing it according to the individual's level of expertise.

Getting grabbed by the hands from behind can be a considerable shock. It is very important to practise regaining your balance.

Use your hip to get the attacker off balance and balance yourself. The stance you end up in will determine your means of attack. Be ready for the attacker trying to grab you by the head.

Without hesitation, attack with your elbows

RELEASES FROM CHOKES

We will now move on to more dangerous holds and grabs, including getting choked from different angles. If our attempts at move and fire, defensive striking and hand releases should fail, this might well be the situation we're facing.

Chokes from the front

If someone gets hold of your throat, there is no time to waste. It is a life-threatening situation and you must do whatever it takes to stop the attack. It is very tricky to train for this circumstance as we must get a sense of urgency without getting injured. One approach is to grab yourself around the throat and see how it feels. You can then repeat this with a partner to establish your threshold before going full force.

Release with plucking motion

The term 'plucking motion' means that we're striking the hand that's around our neck. Far too often we see fingers being used for this motion, but in the heat of the moment fingers tend to slip and slide, especially when the neck is relaxed. It is a curious reaction that if someone grabs you hard by the neck it 'shrinks' and your shoulders come up to lessen the pain. That is part of the solution. Using the hand as a hook, strike that hook against the attacker's hand while hitting his/her neck with the other, free hand. Anchor, balance, attack is the key theme to apply.

Release by controlling the choking arm

When our combat mindset turns from white to red, or even black, in a fraction of a second, especially if we have been taken off balance, it is our natural reaction to make a grab. While doing this we'll also protect our head from getting hit by an incoming punch or headbutt. This takes advantage of the natural reaction to move forward diagonally and simultaneously attack with a knee kick. This is the same movement that happens when being pulled towards the attacker from the side.

Using your hand like a hook to pull the attacker's hand off your throat needs body rotation. To help this, strike with your front hand.

When the choke has turned into something almost like a headlock, go with the flow and remember: anchor, balance and attack.

Using leverage, start attacking with your knees and continue as needed.

Release with arm strike

When your head is forced upwards, the natural reaction is to try to escape the hold by turning. The basis of this release comes from adding a downwards elbow strike to that motion. Try using environmental constraints, such as a wall close behind the defender, to help you understand how this movement develops naturally. You can also resort to the one-hand plucking motion to take control of the arm if their hip moves back far enough.

Side elbow and side hammer punch attacks after the release may create enough space to continue with a side kick. It is important to execute these movements in a row, like chain attacks, making sure the attacker has no time to recuperate. Any defensive strikes and counter-attacks that the attacker then introduces will require new solutions. You must be extremely careful, however, as it then becomes an exercise very prone to causing injuries.

Release from the side, moving out

We have already seen how to react when being pulled towards an attacker from the side. We now come to what to do when the

Feeling the pressure on your neck and throat makes your head turn away from the pain. While your body moves backwards the hand is lifted. We'll use that body motion to turn defence into an attack.

Make the release by striking downwards with the elbow. Once the attacker pushes even slightly, the defender's body will become attuned to the movement. Keep on moving and attacking as the attacker has not yet been injured. Try a hammer punch or side kick and then get away.

Use the attacker's body motion to pull in your hooked hand for the strike. Should the elbow not hit the chin, continue attacking with any opportunity that becomes available, such as a hammer punch or side kick.

first feeling is being pushed the other way. Again, when we feel the hands around our neck squeezing our throat, the head wants to turn away. This brings our shoulder up to hit the attacker's bicep. Our first thought must be to strike and force the attacker off balance. As we move away and strike to the groin, the attacker's chin comes down and that is where we hit with our elbow. Don't worry if we miss, since now we can find a way to make our next attack.

Training tip

Start the training session with the defender's head turned in the opposite direction. The attacker then grabs and pushes from the throat.

RELEASES FROM BEHIND

There are two main responses from the chokeholds from the rear:

- a lifting motion leading to a plucking motion
- a pulling and pushing motion leading to a release with your arm.

There are also solutions that use other directions of movement, but basically the starting point is either to pluck the attacker's hand or use your own hand in a sweeping motion. Again there are tens of variations depending on how the attacker is moving and behaving, but they all come down to anchor, balance and attack.

Stepping forward diagonally from behind

This technique is built on the natural reaction to curl up your shoulders when startled. Whether it is against a push or a pull, we must get used to operating our body from that balance. The problem comes when we try to stand up tall and turn, which is anatomically impossible. Once again, the biggest problem in training comes from an inactive attacker doing nothing more than trying to grab the defender. This can be fixed by making the situation active.

Once you feel the push from the neck and your balance is taken forward, regain your balance by lifting your arm to attack with a hammer punch while turning.

Using the plucking motion from the rear

This defence is another technique that needs the attacker's full involvement. If he/she offers little resistance it takes a very long time to get all the movements right. We need fast solutions that emerge naturally.

The photos here will show how to use one's bodyweight to get back on balance and force the attacker off theirs. This can be trained quickly by using a wall in front of the defender. The attacker forces the defender against the wall. It is the defender who effects the release. It will be clear from the start what to do.

Using the arms release from behind technique, lower your hips, move away backwards from the line of fire diagonally and start striking.

Now hit upwards with your elbow and continue attacking with the initiative you have just taken, perhaps turning towards the attacker's hand you are holding or using a back kick to send him backwards. When turning to make a back kick, however, make sure that he can't grab you by the hair.

11 HAIR GRABS, HEADLOCKS AND BEAR HUGS

HAIR GRABS

Getting grabbed by your hair is a shocking sensation. It is not very pleasant to practise, I've been told, but it is essential to understanding how fast, strong and intense these attacks can be. Again, start by grabbing your hair and start yanking it up and down, side to side. You will immediately feel how your neck muscles start to work. It is then time to find your threshold with the help of a partner. This isn't a problem for people with very short hair or none, but they can get some idea of the feeling by having their neck manipulated..

One thing that becomes very clear immediately is that you can't take your time: every movement must happen at once. To take away the attacker's advantage we must close in and trap his/her arm so that it can't move freely. Then you must attack to injure. Hair grabbing is a very natural form of attack and it can be very effective.

From behind

The surprise, shock and rapid pain that this attack brings are its greatest advantages. Before we even understand what has happened we might be on the floor getting kicked and punched. As soon as you feel the attack, your hands will go where it hurts, so trapping the attacker's arm.

Move in with your hip, just as in the other attacks from behind described previously, to take the attacker off balance and start attacking to injure the groin, chin or solar plexus. Keep moving and attacking. Once you feel the attacker's grip weakening, keep on attacking until there is enough distance between you to help you recuperate and assess the situation.

Getting grabbed by the hair from behind is a shock. To ease the pain, move in the direction of the pull and attack at the same time.

Resorting to behaviour learned to deal with being grabbed from behind will help in the search for attacking solutions.

From the side

As Hedi's expression suggests, this attack is not among her favourite exercises. The solution is the same as being grabbed from behind: trap (anchor), close in and attack (balance and attack), attack and attack until there is no longer a threat. The key to success is using elbows and knees to keep the attacker constantly off balance and force them to move backwards. Once you feel their grip weakening, attack to gain control of the situation.

Training to deal with hair grabs is painful, but it is essential. As soon as you feel you are being pulled with a tight grip, instantly place your hand on the attacker's and stop it moving you around.

As you move forward towards the attacker, a straightforward elbow strike becomes a natural way to continue the attack.

From the front

The biggest issue with the front attack is that when the attacker is pushing you down he might try to knee kick you in the face. Again, the solution is to trap his hand and then move forward with your hands held as a type of shield. Use your forearms to punch the attacker's jaw and face, while being aware that he might try to hit your body with the other hand, although there is not much you can do about that.

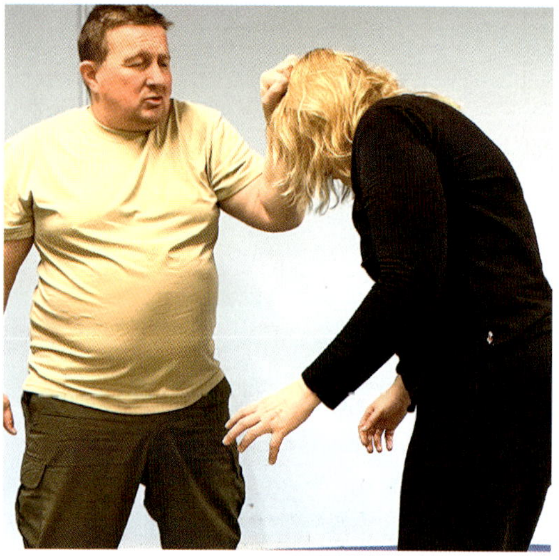

The pain from someone grabbing your hair can be excruciating, but the answer is to go with the pull and turn that movement into an attack.

Start by delivering a double elbow punch to the face while anchoring the attacker's hand. You should then shake your head towards the grabbing hand and hit with your body until your hair is released.

HEADLOCKS

Headlocks come in different forms and directions with various hand positions. The big issue is that when the arms are blocking the circulation, unconsciousness can come in seconds. It is important to understand few principles:

- Anchoring: we must take away the attacker's ability to move freely.
- Balancing: we must regain our balance while taking the attacker off balance.
- Attacking to injure: we need to injure the attacker.

The emphasis should be on the concept of 'not a single wasted movement', with the focus on the attack, not the release. We must also properly assess the attacker's intentions, not just take a hold and stand there. This is where non-linear teaching methods, task simplification, CLA tools and the schema theory are essential approaches to learning. Unfortunately, thanks to the long history of the linear teaching methods, information processing theory is still used widely. Even though it might feel that we're picking things up in training, the reality is different. You would again be wise to vary your approach and focus on the attacker's intentions.

We will start by examining a few different approaches an attacker may attempt from the side, rear and front.

From the side (pulling low)

The side headlock is often seen in real life. Tens of solutions are suggested online but very few of these describe the attacker's intentions, focusing instead on step-by-step descriptions of defensive movements, when really the solution once more is to move as one: anchor, balance, attack. Let's look at a few from the point of view of the attacker's intention.

In the sequence illustrated my intention is to pull Hedi down to the ground in a headlock. To prevent that happening she must get used to moving in close, her hip against my hip, and her free leg in between my legs. The natural reaction, however, would be to try to pull backwards, and then it would all be down to strength alone.

While performing this motion, she's also attacking by punching me in the groin and then immediately lifting her head up. If I can manage to keep her head down, however, she will be going to the ground.

If she has spent her time in training simply focusing on where her hands ought to be, that is what she will do in a real-life event and there is no way she could prevent me taking her down. If, however, her focus is on anchoring herself to me, regaining her balance and getting me off balance, her hands will naturally fall into place. The technique itself is never exactly the same, which is why understanding the key tasks – anchor, balance, attack – are so important.

Training tips

- Make sure that you have a soft mat to land on.
- Start by exploring the best ways to anchor, balance and attack.
- Simplify the exercise by placing your hands on the target and keeping them there.
- As you make the exercise harder, remember that failing is one aspect of learning.

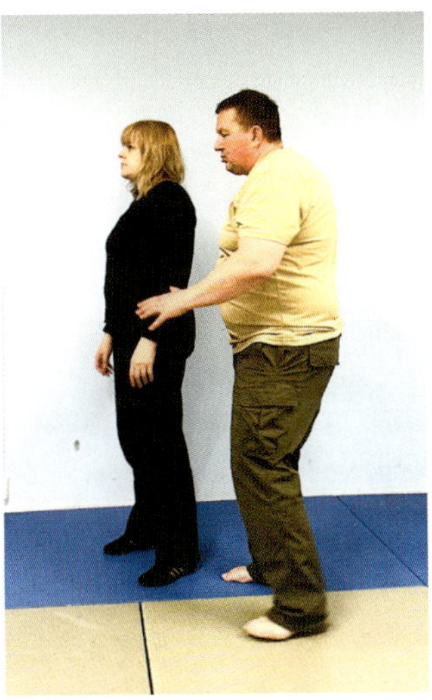

Side headlock starting position. To increase the element of surprise when training, the defender could be looking forward or even to the other side when the attack begins.

The defender's main task when being pulled forward and down is to hit in with her hips, strike to the groin and pull the attacker's head up. This will vary from one attack to another. Where to pull is not important, but what it hopes to achieve.

Once you have gained the initiative, attack the closest target with full force, following up on every available target.

From the side (high)

The way to avoid getting caught in a side headlock is to make use of a slip and punch before you get locked. As shown here I can't get hold of Hedi's head because she has already started attacking my face with both hands, immediately taking me off balance. Once she has created the momentum to punch, she takes advantage of it. Pay attention to anchoring, hip to hip, and then move on to balancing and attacking. If I were to get my hand around her neck, she already knows the movement solution from previous exercises. Train all these moves together and throw in all sorts of variations.

Side headlock reactive defence. In case the attacker gets a strong hold of you, we must train to be able to notice the attack as soon as possible. Here Hedi reacts immediately to the hand wrapping around her neck by attacking.

From the side (pulling down)

In order to avoid being thrown, especially when one's legs are blocked from anchoring to the attacker, there is only one direction to go and that is backwards. That's not an optimal solution, but as Imi Lichtenfeld said, 'do what you can'. The key point is to move to an angle that your opponent can't follow and then put your buttocks to the ground while anchoring yourself around the attacker. For a wrestler that's just another day at the office, but a regular person should train for this very carefully to avoid injury. As a first step let's simplify the movement and make the landing soft.

You can vary the attack by not giving the defender an opportunity to step forward. By making the defender feel that they will be thrown over the hip in a second, this increases the defender's urgency to anchor, balance and attack. To do so, Hedi takes a hold like a bear hug and hits me at the hips with her hip, sending my balance forward and so stopping me making the throw. Continuing with the turning motion, she can now force me off balance and sweep me off to the side. Then it is time to move out.

It is important to train to counter different types of approach by the attacker. Here I'm preventing Hedi from stepping in and making her feel that she is about to be thrown over.

The best way of taking me off balance would be for Hedi to get a hold of me and pull herself close at the same time. She can then continue the movement and let me land on my side.

From the front (stepping through)

This movement is often referred to as the guillotine hold. The solution depends on how we feel the attacker is moving his/her body: are they pushing us down with their body, trying to land on top of us or are they pulling us up and trying to choke us right there.

In this case I have grabbed Hedi by the head and am preparing to pull her up. As she feels this movement, she turns sideways immediately, getting hold of my arms and pushing her head through the opening in my armpit.

When she gets to my side, she has a strong hold of my arm and she could quite easily hit my hand with all her weight, forcing my body to move down. The other option would be to keep moving and deliver a side kick to my leg, breaking my knee.

Training tips

- Make the attacker exaggerate his/her movement and pull the defender with him/her to complete the technique.
- Focus on the defender's intention to lift the attacker's head by leaning strongly against their body with his/her back while doing so.
- Simplify the movement by already placing the defender's hands on the hand of the attacker.
- Be extra careful when completing the kick to the knee as it will break.

The natural reaction when an attacker is pulling you up with a front headlock is to grab their hands before stepping through while moving forward diagonally.

Once you have moved through it's time to attack.

Seeing the opportunity to use a side kick to my knee, Hedi uses it immediately to break my structure.

From the front (attacking forward)

Should the attacker pull the defender strongly towards himself, the defender will have a hard time trying to step through. The attacker's intention might be to push the defender to the ground on her face. The defensive motion that emerges from the attacker's movement is to move strongly forward by punching with the attacker's head side of shoulder forward, making him/her move even further backwards and off balance. The movement is coupled by striking him/her to the groin and then immediately bringing your shoulder upwards. This action might hit the attacker on the chin, but the key thing is to have the ability to turn your hand to hit the attacker's throat. Hitting the throat will create enough space to pull your head out while the attacker is moving backwards. A common manoeuvre after this is to continue attacking with a front kick.

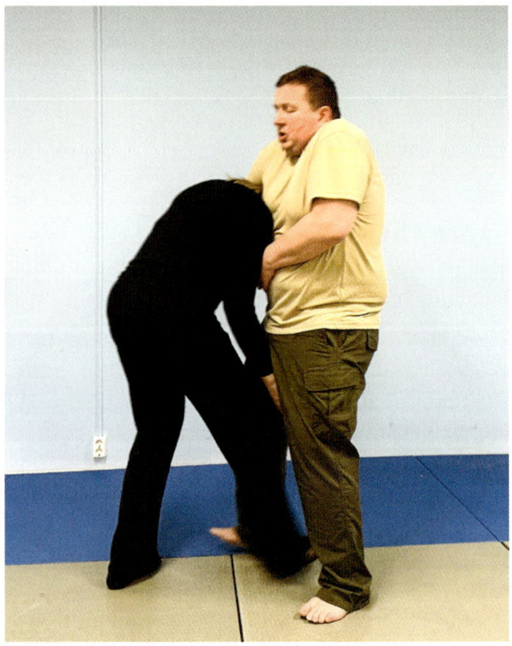

When being dragged or pulled a front headlock will prevent the defender from stepping through. If that is the attacker's intention, you must resort to attacking and making space with them.

Once a hit to the groin has brought the attacker's head down, the hand that delivered the punch moves up with the elbow, making the head move backwards and leaving the throat open to an attack.

Headlocks from behind

The rear-naked choke is another very typical headlock that is meant to hold and choke a person unconscious. Once it's locked, only seconds remain to protect the large blood veins in one's neck as well as the windpipe from crushing. Everything has to be done in one motion.

The starting point of the defence training is the attacker's intention. Should the defender's first movement be towards the attacker's holding hand side, that's the way to move. This is exactly the movement we looked at when discussing the choke from the side, which is a similar problem and similar solution. On the other hand, if the first reaction is to turn away from the incoming hand, that must be the direction of the defence. Sometimes the attack is so rapid that once the defender starts moving in one direction, the attacker's motions send her moving in another. Find ways to solve the problem in training and vary the attacker's movement and intention while doing so. Headlocks are very dangerous attacks and everything happens very quickly. The key problem encountered in training is that the slow pace of movements make it difficult to train against and with the shock. It takes a lot from both the attacker and the defender to make the training as real as possible in a safe manner.

Our first response to a headlock from behind is to turn away from the incoming hand. We must make that turn our first attacking movement. Note that here I'm standing on a green-grey mat.

A stomping kick to my knee will now break my balance and structure.

Hedi's continuing attack has moved me backwards to the blue mat. By keeping me off balance she has a chance to release and use the kicking solution.

BEAR HUGS

Bear hugs are used to stop movement and throw or take down the target. Different variations of bear hugs come in many forms and so it is important to train for many types of attack. Once again the main problem is the slow pace and the need to break the movement step by step with results that do not give a true representation of the intensity of the grips and the attacker's intentions. You first need to get used to the effect of being shaken and taken off balance, as well as how it feels to be thrown. Safe falling is needed here. In this chapter we'll look at how bear hugs are used to start attacks from the front, side and rear, and with hands free or locked.

From the front (arms free)

We'll start with a situation where the attacker gets hold of you from the front, but your hands are free. You may remember the photo of Hedi distracted by her phone in Chapter 6. I then saw an opportunity to grab her and drag her away. The next photo shows how she re-established her balance while simultaneously striking me on the side of the neck. Once she succeeds in taking me off balance, she immediately continues with kicking and punching to create space.

In this situation you might find your hand in various positions, while remaining free of the attacker's hold. The key point is to use the hands to strike and disrupt the attacker's balance, while maintaining or regaining one's own balance. Try different ways to get the same result. Remember, when you're hitting someone in the face in training, don't get injured. It is the same with the neck. Helmets with faceguards have their place, but a continuous, deliberate movement performed in slow motion works wonders.

From the front (arms locked)

Let's move on to a situation where the attacker succeeds in locking the target's hands. Again, the situation starts from the target not being aware of the danger and the ambush seems to succeed.

The principle we will again be using is anchor, balance and attack, all happening almost simultaneously, not one stage at a time. It is important to remember that if the attacker moves in strongly, making the defender take a step back and turn sideways or diagonally sideways, the defence changes. You will get this technique to emerge by attacking with a drag and pull.

As I startle her, Hedi takes advantage of the startle-flinch by bending her knees, tucking her chin into her chest and placing her hands so as to push away the danger. Note that the phone is still in her hand.

Continuing her attack, Hedi keeps her head down to increase power in her abdominal muscles. using her forearms to hit the side of my neck.

Bear hug from the front with hands locked. As soon as you feel the attacker's hands closing in, strike and make room for yourself to take the attacker off balance.

Keep on moving and use the side position to strike.

From the front (attacker's head low)

The attacker's intention is to dive down and either pin the defender against an obstacle or lift her off her feet. This may well lead to a takedown as well. The attacker's movement takes the defender backwards and this is the movement we must take advantage of and make it a part of the defence.

Use the attacker's motion to move, trying to keep the attacker's head in front of you, while striking with your bicep to the back of the attacker's head.

From the side (arms closed)

The attacker's intention dictates the defence, which has similar problems as chokes from the side and uses the same defensive movements. When moving towards the attacker, anchor, balance and attack in that direction, and when being pushed do the same but in the opposite way. How you continue is up to the feedback received from the attacker's movements.

Everything is happening at once – grabbing and pulling, an elbow punch to the rear, moving the attacker's head backwards while turning your body and causing him to be taken off balance.

Resorting to the solutions already familiar from the discussion of headlocks, hit to the face and continue as suggested by the feedback.

A bear hug from the side when the attacker is pulling is just like a choke from the side. Move in and take the attacker off balance.

Continuing the attack. I have here come to realise that I am about to get kicked to the groin, so I'm trying to pull my hips back, a defensive action that is helping Hedi maintain the initiative.

Hedi now has the side position, and she has locked my shoulder. She can now continue by either putting me on the ground by squeezing the lock or use the more drastic solution of knee kicking me to the head. The situation dictates the best operational and legal solution.

I have attacked with a pushing motion and now have my hands around Hedi's waist and hands. She has taken advantage of my movement to pull me towards her as her elbow is coming to meet my chin.

The elbow may have caused me to lose consciousness, but Hedi makes sure that I won't be able to follow her by placing a side kick on my knee.

Bear hugs from behind

The last general direction from which bear hugs may come is attacks from behind. These are very similar to those involving headlocks, hand grabbing and choking that come from the same direction. Nothing changes from the practising point of view: the attacker needs to have intention and a task to do. Using non-linear teaching methods, CLA and representative practice design, the defences will become apparent and all the basic techniques will emerge.

Arms free

The obvious solution to all situations where the defender's arms are free is to use them to anchor, balance and attack. The attacker's intention to drag the defender away from the scene is the starting point of our investigation on the subject.

There will also be situations where the attacker's intention is to lift the defender and either throw them to the ground and keep on attacking them on the spot or just carry them away.

From the rear (arms closed)

In situations where our arms are closed tightly in the attacker's grip the opportunities to strike with our hands are limited, so we'll need to resort to other means of attack. One of the key requirements is to anchor strongly and take away the attacker's balance. In many techniques we are presented with solutions that involve stomping kicks, but from experience I can say that you shouldn't take your feet off the solid ground.

The body movements might have numerous similarities with headlock-type attacks. These need to be explored in training. Again, there must be an intention to the attack for the solutions to emerge, applying the core principles.

In the next chapter we'll look at throws, sweeps and takedowns as these might sometimes emerge as viable solutions to de-escalate the situation. If we can get the attacker to fall on the ground, that gives us more time to get away.

When the attacker's intention is to drag the defender away, the high hold is very effective once the attacker gets the defender off balance.

By anchoring onto the attacker's hand while regaining her balance, the defender is denying the attacker the ability to release his hands and change the attack, while getting herself to a good position from which to deliver effective strike.

One solution is to attack with elbow punches while maintaining control of the attacker's arm. You can continue from there as the situation unfolds.

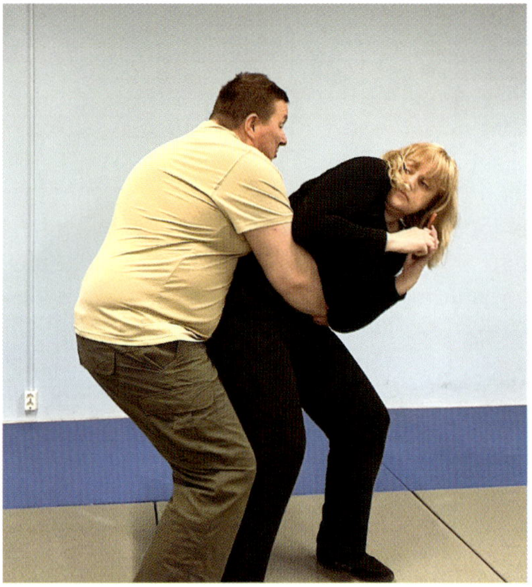

The immediate response to the low bear hug is the startle-flinch down. Here we need to emphasise that the hands are held together. Hedi has her phone in her hands and this makes a good constraint to ensure her elbows are holding my hands tightly.

Hedi is still attacking me with her elbows, creating space and attempting to force a release. My head is high since I'm about to throw her backwards, making my face an open target.

After the elbow punches have forced me to open my hands, Hedi continues to distract and disorientate me using hammer punches. A natural continuation from this position would be a side kick to add further distance.

A situation where a bear hug is used to trap the hands might lead to you being dragged away or thrown down. The sudden rush of adrenaline will make all the muscles feel tense at once and that is what we'll need to use to our advantage. Note that this needs to be experienced in training.

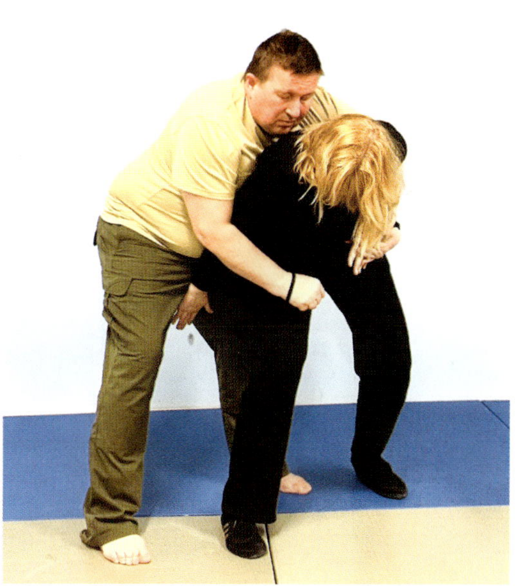

As soon as possible, find a way to attack. If you can use your hands, use them. Don't just hit the groin, grab it and pull! This will make the attacker's head tilt upwards and give him a strong incentive to let go. Keep holding on to at least one arm to prevent him from changing the attack.

It is time to start using the advantage you just gained, perhaps using elbow punches, a back kick or even perhaps turn to the side of the hand that you're holding. Always Be Contacting and continue attacking.

You have been here before, so repeat what you've done before and keep on repeating the outcome.

12 THROWING, SWEEPING AND OTHER TAKEDOWNS

Bear hugs, alongside the headlocks, form the basis of grappling in combat skills. Coupled with control of the hands and taking the target off balance they are the basis for a range of sweeps and throws, which combine bear hugs, headlocks and striking. You will come to learn how to do these when practising attacking moves, headlocks and bear hugs.

A detailed discussion of these would need a whole new book, but we'll look at a few basic principles and tips, especially those that ensure training is safe, as it is important to understand how to train for these attacks. This will then lead us to ground fighting, the environment we definitely want to avoid and where we need to get back on our feet as soon as possible.

LEARNING TO LAND

One of the key parts of practising the throws and takedowns is to make sure that people are safe in landings, or breakfalls, whichever term you prefer when talking about hitting the ground.

It may seem odd to start by feeling the surface as your hands hit the floor, but this action raises a few issues:

- The commonest injury from a fall is to break your wrists.
- Hands will fly back naturally due to the velocity of the movement.

One exercise to help you learn how to land is to allow your partner to lift you up and then drop you. Scale the height and learn how to take the hit.

Meeting Mother Earth

As a horse owner and rider, I have fallen off quite a few times. Once this was caused by a low-hanging branch (luckily that was onto soft snow). Once the saddle came loose and rolled over to the side. Once the horse fell on her side on ice. And a few times I have been bucked off.

The common factor in all these mishaps is that the startle-flinch kicked in to protect my head in the best way possible. The only parts of my body that have been injured so far have been my forearms and wrists after I hit a perfect landing strike, as learned in ju-jitsu thirty years ago, when the saddle buckle came loose and I was thrown off, but the frozen surface of the training field, churned up by hoofprints, didn't work like a tatami mat. It felt like coming down at speed from a hip throw and my hand just flew out. When my horse fell on her side I just flew off like a rocket. Luckily I was using a western saddle with wide stirrups, so my foot didn't get stuck. But the landing was face forward, lifting my head up and making my knees and hands take the force of the impact. No harm was done and the snowy surface also helped. Most importantly the horse was unharmed. The point is that we need to train to be able to land at speed safely by any means possible. There is no sense in trying to break the landing into small parts, but you must practise getting to the landing position immediately.

Riding Hartland Queen of Hearts, 'Hertta', in winter 2017. Learning how to fall is just as important for a horseman as learning how not to fall. Here, just as in Krav Maga, we must learn how to maintain and regain our balance in order to stay upright. Many self-defence situations end up on the ground, but that is not the only option.

- The head is the most important part of the body to protect.
- The speed we'll be landing at is fast. It's not as though we're sitting down gently.

Instead of emphasising how hard to hit the ground with your hands, we must focus on protecting the 'computer'. As the landing is fast, start by landing on soft surfaces and then familiarise your body with harder surfaces.

Starting by using a soft surface to land on allows us to experience the takedown at full speed. This reduces unwanted injuries and enables the instructors and coaches to start placing the constraints needed to make the movement solution (or technique) safe and well constructed. Once we start putting the emphasis on training the landing from various angles and takedowns, incorporating the attacker's intention to continue attacking, our focus of attention is taken away from the breakfall and put on the more important task of stopping the attacker's intentions.

When moving on to the throws and takedowns, use non-linear teaching methods, the CLA and representative practice design to help us understand the situations in which a throw or takedown would be a natural continuation to a defensive action.

OVER-THE-LEG THROW

In Krav Maga we use our natural reactions to allow the techniques to emerge. The over-the-leg throw is a natural body movement with the opponent attached to one's body. Using a non-linear approach, start from the position where the actual throw happens and then make the movement.

The over-the-leg throw as an attack is something that a stronger and bigger attacker might try. When attempting a throw or take-down it is necessary to get our opponent off balance. Here I am using a hand pull and fore-arm punch to Hedi's neck to take her off balance. While doing this, I move my leg in front of hers to stop her taking a balancing step. This will make her fall.

Using a soft mat when practising the over-the-leg throw makes it possible to repeat the fall and the outcome without injuring yourself. The mat doesn't only provide a soft landing, it also helps get the thrower's foot in the safe position, with the heel upwards. The thrower's task is to keep your partner attached to your body and hit your heel to the side of the mat.

The over-the-leg throw can also be used as an attack. It is here being launched from a headlock hold.

OUTSIDE SWEEP

The outside sweep means that both of the opponent's legs are swept away from outside his/her posture. It can be done either forward and when turning backwards. This movement is not simple, but once you find turning natural the leg sweep is easy to couple with the turning motion. In order to make the attacker fall we must disrupt the attacker's body balance, forcing her shoulders to a line outside her hips and legs.

When training for this move it helps to wear judo jackets to simplify the motion and make falls more comfortable.

Outside sweep performed while turning from a pushing front choke attack.

INSIDE SWEEP

The inside sweep movement means that our leg is being used between the opponent's legs to sweep their base leg away. In the situation shown here the attacker starts with a haymaker punch. The defender's response is a stabbing attacking-defence movement coupled with a reverse roundhouse kick between the legs.

Outside sweep performed from a pushing side choke attack.

Inside sweep performed from a punching defence situation.

FRONT TAKEDOWN

The front takedown is often seen in combat sports, in which it is used to bring the opponent down. Attacks of this type also appear in real-life self-defence contexts. It is a feasible self-defence technique for situations such as the one illustrated, in which Hedi starts with a haymaker punch to my head. I am using the technique of moving forward with a rear hand punch (*see* Chapter 6), but instead of punching, I take hold of her leg and bring her down.

Front takedown following a punch defence.

SUMMARY

Learning how to land is an important skill, especially in those parts of the world where it gets slippery in winter. Learning how to balance oneself on a slippery surface is a great exercise for those who might have to experience a real-life simulation a number of times every winter. Hitting your hands on ice and concrete a few times is a magical constraint that steers the focus towards protecting your head and hands on landing.

We must learn how to defend against different grappling attacks and in this way we will also learn how to use them. This is why in Krav Maga training it is very important to sometimes train with grappling coaches from mixed martial arts, judo and wrestling. Every instructor must know the fundamentals of takedowns and throws in order to teach the defences. Training can't be representative if the attacks that we're training to defend against are not done properly. It is important to understand, however, that the mindset for Krav Maga training is different. We're not there to fight five-minute rounds. We're there to hit and move away. Using exercise models in which once the defender gets up, he/she may be taken down again by another attacker makes it more representative and offers the opportunity to use other defensive tools following the principle of move and fire. Using time constraints of between five and twenty seconds to get off the ground is an excellent way of reinforcing that, in a self-defence context, we simply can't stay down. In the next chapter we'll move on to the ground fighting.

13 GROUND FIGHTING

Fighting on the ground and from the ground are essential self-defence skills. We may not want to end up on the ground, but sometimes that is what we need to do. In this chapter we'll look at how to use the Krav Maga principles from different positions and at different stages of the combat mindset.

ACTION CAPACITIES ON THE GROUND

Learning how to use the surface to balance oneself, how to move and fire from different body positions and then adding the opponent player to the game are the key elements in training. As our perception changes from being visual to more about the senses, so our comprehension of the concept of anchoring, balance and attack will become different.

We'll need to learn how to punch and kick both from and on the ground from different positions and angles. While doing so, we'll need to learn to use body formations like arching our backs (bridging), putting our knees and feet between ourselves and the opponent, and using our hands and legs like scissors to immobilise or unbalance the opponent, while retaining our own balance.

This requires good core muscles and coordination. It doesn't matter how many sit-ups you can do since the movements on the ground are so different. For this purpose, many games focusing on different forms of attention are available, very much like those used in other grappling arts. In Krav Maga the self-defence context requires that we introduce to the exercises time constraints and the task of getting up. That is why we start off by learning attacking from the ground, focusing on being able to get up while our partner is trying to push us back down.

The YouTube video 'Training Drills for Takedowns and Ground Work | Self Defense & MMA Tips' (https://youtu.be/g-R1hDEswFE) will provide valuable ideas for your drills.

THE STRAIGHTEST WAY IS THE BEST WAY

In Krav Maga the aim is to keep movements and techniques as straightforward and simple as possible. The challenge comes from the surroundings, the ground, the individuals and the tasks we'll need to complete. The slightest change in an attacker's movements, size differences and other factors are all elements we'll need to focus on. That is why it is so important to stay focused on the outcome and not spend too much time on small, technical details that can be fixed with active attacker resistance training. In the end it all comes down to understanding a few movements and principles and being able to put them together in any order needed to stop the attacker's intentions.

The baseline movements that we'll need to work with are bridging, shrimping and the scissors sweep. It is important to understand how the joints move and when they won't move any more without breaking. We already know that we can attack the head, the body and the legs. It is the same in ground fighting. As we don't want to end up on the ground, we'll need to focus on getting up as soon as we can.

Time and distance are extremely important factors when you're on the ground. Since we don't have much time to focus just on ground survival, the training needs to be as representative as possible, focusing on the basics, and then add aspects of CLA and representative practice design to improve the results. We will start by exploring the foundations of moving on the ground and then getting up.

Shrimping means turning sideways and bringing your knees or even feet between the attacker and yourself.

Bridging, or arching, means getting your hips off the ground while moving the opponent over the top. This takes the attacker off balance and uses their own body movement to support the defence.

The scissors sweep can be done either with your legs or hands. The key is to prevent the opponent's movement to the side where the cutting limb is moving.

GETTING UP FROM THE GROUND

The situation dictates the most appropriate movement for getting up as quickly as you can. It also depends on your individual action capacity. In the context of self-defence two practical methods are taught. The first of these is using your hand as a base to move your leg behind to the kneeling position and then standing up. This requires a bit of flexibility and naturally a solid surface, certainly no ice or gravel under your hand. It is feasible to use in situations where there is enough space between you and the threat. It can also be employed when you are holding something, perhaps a pistol or an object that can be used as a defensive tool.

The other method is much less complicated. Roll on your side and use both hands on the ground to give support. It is crucial to get up as steadily as possible and ready to attack at any moment. The situations are not clear and simple, so dynamic training is needed to make these choices fluent.

Getting up from the ground using one arm as a supporting point and then moving your leg behind to stand up.

Standard ground defence position makes it possible to strike and move on the ground.

Tactical getting up.

Getting up by turning on your side with both hands supporting and being ready to attack gives a more solid base for attacks or defences.

ATTACKING FROM THE GROUND

Learning how to use different kicks and punches while on the ground is where we start in Krav Maga ground fighting. Just as when we are standing, observe the principle of move and fire.

Our main goal is to get our legs between us and the attacker. Then continue kicking, preferably below the knee, to prevent the attacker getting hold of our legs or defending against the kicks.

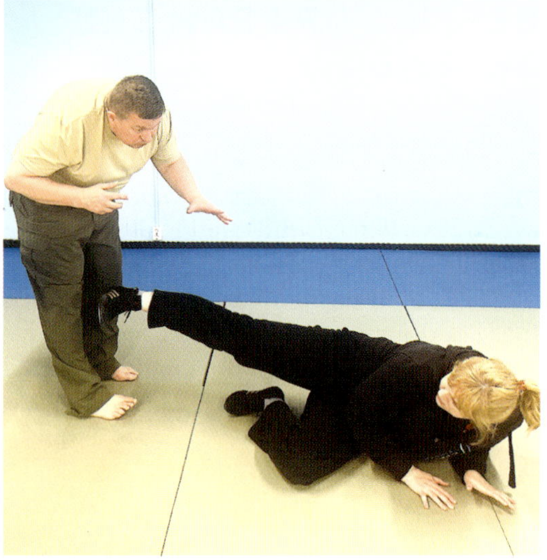

Continue from the stomping kick to a side kick while getting ready to either attack again or retreat and get up.

A stomping kick from the ground targeted at the attacker's knee gives room to get up safely.

Defending with a roundhouse kick from the ground sends the attacker backwards.

DEFENDING AGAINST KICKS

Now that we've established the basis of defence from the ground, let's move on to situations in which we'll need to strike defensively before being able to attack ourselves. We will start with occasions when the attacker is using kicking from a distance as the first line of attack. Since we understand how dangerous a kick may be if we get hit, it is vital that the training exercises should be as representative as possible, but never ignoring safety.

Defence against a roundhouse kick to the head

The attacker's intention here is to deliver a football kick to the defender's head. To start

Defence against roundhouse kick to the head.

practising the full-speed kicks, use a kick pad to represent the kicking leg and a focus pad on the attacker's chest and shoulder to provide a kicking target for a full-speed counter from the defender. As with any kicking, the importance of shooting the knee first and then letting the shin and foot do the rest with a whip-like motion is the key.

As part of action capacity training, delivering roundhouse kicks while lying on one's side, and even performing some mobility and flexibility exercises from that position, play an important role in helping the body to understand what is required. CLA training methodology can be employed using rings or smaller pads to hit the target and then move on to getting the defender used to the aggression and speed.

When you start training for the skill with a partner, always use proper protective gear. The defender needs a helmet with both a facial and mouth guard, groin protection, shin protectors and perhaps some forearm guards to reduce the impact. Boxing gloves may also be used to protect the hands, but some think they limit the movement too much. The attacker needs the same gear in order to make near full-speed simulations possible. The psychological safety that comes from trusting your training partner is vital.

The attacker needs to have a clear picture in their head about the intentions they need to represent. As seen in real-life situations the first kick may be a roundhouse kick to the head. It may then continue with either more kicks from the side towards the head and/or body or turn into stomping kicks towards the head. It may also end up in a crazy assault, just aggressively jumping on the victim.

Defence against a stomping kick to the head

The stomping kick towards the head is not easy to train with a partner in a representative way since it requires the attacker to use full weight on the kicks. Once the weight is

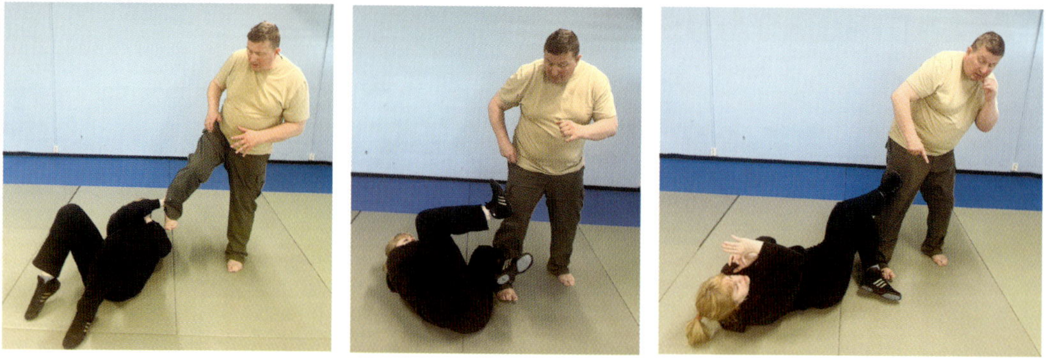

Defence against stomping kick.

loaded, it is very hard to stop the movement if the defender freezes. This can be solved safely in training, however, by using kick pads or foam rollers to represent the stomping leg.

The defender might be able to move out from the line of attack and turn their feet in between to attack, but sometimes it happens that the leading hand defence becomes trapped between the attacker's legs, requiring the defender to move away quickly. Whether this movement means sliding behind the attacker or using their legs to sprawl out the attacker's legs depends on how the defender assesses the situation. Creating action capacity to permit both options is a great warm-up.

Defence against a low roundhouse kick to the body

Learning defences against roundhouse-type kicks to the body is easier from the safety point of view than those aimed at the head. We can use the same kind of constraints to focus the attention as well as the same protective gear. Using the shin to kick in the defence like standing up is easy to apply. When working with a kick pad to represent the target to be kicked, we can practise without shin protectors, but when moving on to repeating this exercise hundreds of times shin on shin, it is sensible to wear protectors.

DEFENDING AGAINST PUNCHES

We will now move on to ground defence that starts closer in from the distance of a straight punch. Working from different positions and stances, we'll need to learn how and when to use the body defence moves mentioned at the start of this chapter: bridging, shrimping and scissors.

Starting from a position where the attacker is on top of you, you will need fast reactions or the punch hitting you will create huge problems. There are multiple techniques you can use to start dealing with the situation, but the most urgent needs are to get the attacker off balance and go on the attack. If you can get close, get close. If you can't, get him off. That's simple, not easy.

When seeking quick training solutions to these situations, it is a good idea to start from the position where the attacker has his knee of the striking side hand up and he loads the hand to the strike. Using sharp vocal cues like shouts while attacking helps the defender take full advantage of their primal startle-flinch response. Once you're ready to move on to that phase of the training it is a good idea to use protective gear like a helmet with a face guard and employ open-palm punching.

Changing the starting position from the mount to guard also changes the opportunities on offer. Using the shrimping movement

Fast and decisive action is needed when the attacker starts to punch from the mount position.

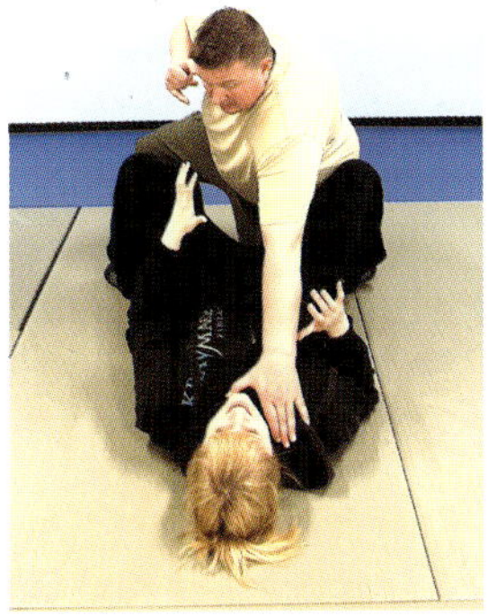

The opportunity to use shrimping as an attack from the open guard position can quickly be learned.

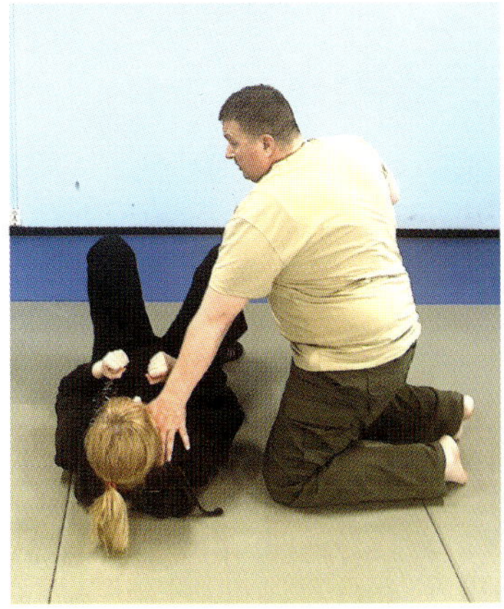

From the side guard, turning your legs in between your opponent's and moving your head away from danger is the fast solution.

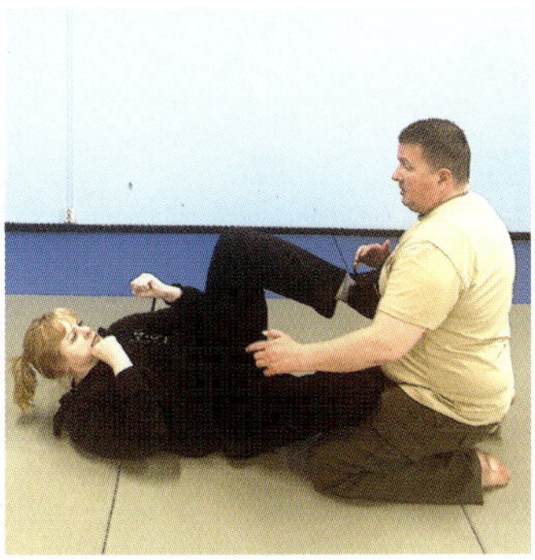

Turn towards the threat and start kicking.

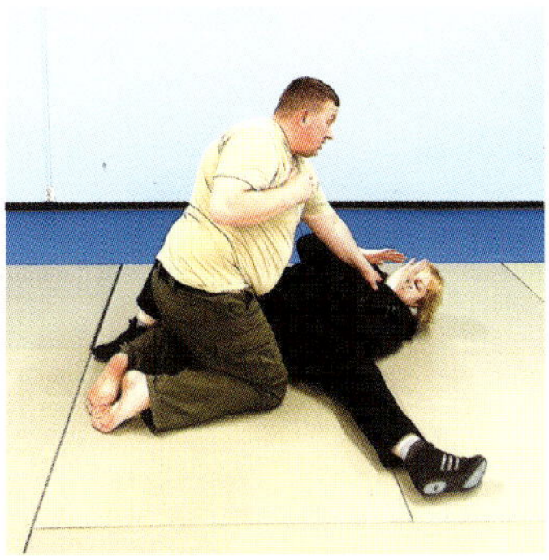

An attempt to use shrimping didn't work and the attacker has closed the distance, so it is time to use the scissors.

The scissors can be used to turn the attacker away from the position and continue defending.

to create distance is effective in this situation and turning to use one's legs and feet as weapons changes the game. However, it is still possible that we miss the target and so the attacker should wear kick pads or body protection when practising full-speed solutions in order to make the training safe and representative.

Should the attacker manage to get closer, and the shrimping motion is no longer a viable choice, you should learn how to use your legs in a scissor-type movement pattern. In this, one side sweeps horizontally, preventing the attacker from holding their balance while the other side strikes a bit higher, with the upper body following the direction. The action capacity needed is the ability to turn on one's stomach while striking with the legs. Training for this requires a combination of timing and force. If the attacker has a high bodyweight, you need to train to make an immediate change from the scissors move to the shrimping move, since even the slightest change in the attacker's base either enables or disables the movement solution.

DEFENCES WITHIN GRAPPLING DISTANCE

As our possibilities of defending ourself on the ground get ever closer, we enter the true weight-class distance. In combat sports this type of situation involves participants of the same weight. This is an important point to consider when we start training in self-defence situations. It is helpful to have same-sized people training together and then start changing the constraints, weight being one, by training with people of a different size.

The basic defensive solution is to use bridging as described above when defending against punches. Here, however, it is the attacker's intention that drives the solution.

The attacker's intention might be to use their hand to create a shoulder lock, which would immobilise the shoulder and thus the whole body if successful. The defender first needs to break the attacker's posture. The defence in the following sequence takes as little as 1.5–2 seconds.

Being pinned down by a heavier attacker choking you on the ground is the time for action. When the attacker's weight is pressing strongly on the defender's throat the only viable option is to hit the attacker's hands in a defensive striking-type movement, and simultaneously bridge and attack.

Once the defender starts the defensive movement there is no turning back. Just keep going. If the movement stops, immediately change direction.

When the release is complete, it is time to move out, turn one's legs in between your opponent's and start kicking.

Before I manage to get the shoulder lock in place, Hedi still has a chance to defend by striking my armpit and driving her elbow downwards at the same time, so releasing the lock.

As she seeks to distract me by attacking my face and eyes with her fingers, Hedi starts to shrimp away.

By managing to free her hips and chest and using her forearm and elbow to strike and push my head and shoulder apart, she stands a chance of getting away.

HEADLOCKS ON THE GROUND

Headlocks on the ground are highly dangerous situations and come in various forms. It is vital to learn how to react in these situations, especially as the attacker varies their intentions. Since even a small change in the attacker's balance and bodyweight forces the defender to change the direction of the movement, these need a lively manner of drilling. In this training format the attacker can enforce the defender's training by giving verbal cues like 'Change direction' or 'Grab my face'. To prevent the defender panicking, keep the pace steady and add speed and pressure as the success rate improves. The defender needs to know how to perform the bridging, shrimping and scissors moves as well as being able to use the rolling motions of the body. The defender must also

The defender is caught in a headlock on the ground, but for a second the attacker has his head up when adjusting his position. This is when the defender needs to move in.

Using the bridging from the hip together with finger strikes to the face.

Twisting the attacker's head to the side while turning her hips, the defender can turn the attacker on his stomach.

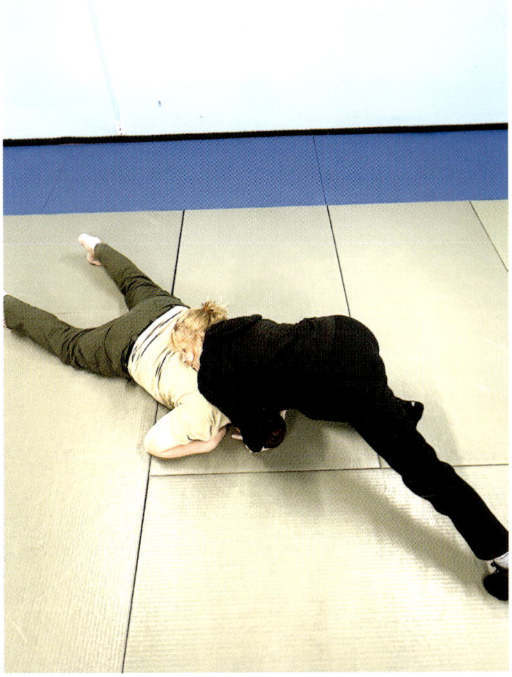

Keeping her chest and head tightly on the attacker's back, the defender pins the attacker to the ground. Keeping control offers her the best possible way to move out.

understand and be able to visualise both players' positions. For instance, it is not physically possible to roll over when the attacker is in a sideways position. If the movements are trained using non-linear teaching methods, task simplification and the constraints-led approach, they should be relatively quick to learn.

Attacker's intention: neck crank

This situation emerges naturally from a side headlock in the standing position that ends on the ground. While there is also a chance that the defender might complete a forward roll while doing this, in this situation the attacker manages to stop the motion and the defender needs to change the direction of the defence.

The attacker is creating a tight lock behind the defender's neck and squeezing it tighter with an arm hold.

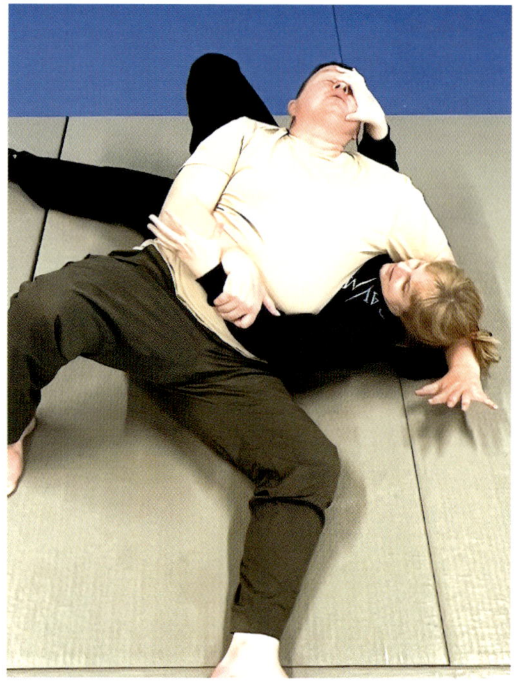

Using a palm strike to the face with the fingers splayed for better grip, the defender is moving her hips out to get the attacker's head to lock.

By using a reverse roundhouse kick to the attacker's jaw and locking her ankles, the defender is getting the attacker into a position where it will be difficult to hold on.

With her ankles locked, the defender straightens her legs by kicking and then pulls back for a roll onto her knees, while maintaining a tight lock around the attacker's neck.

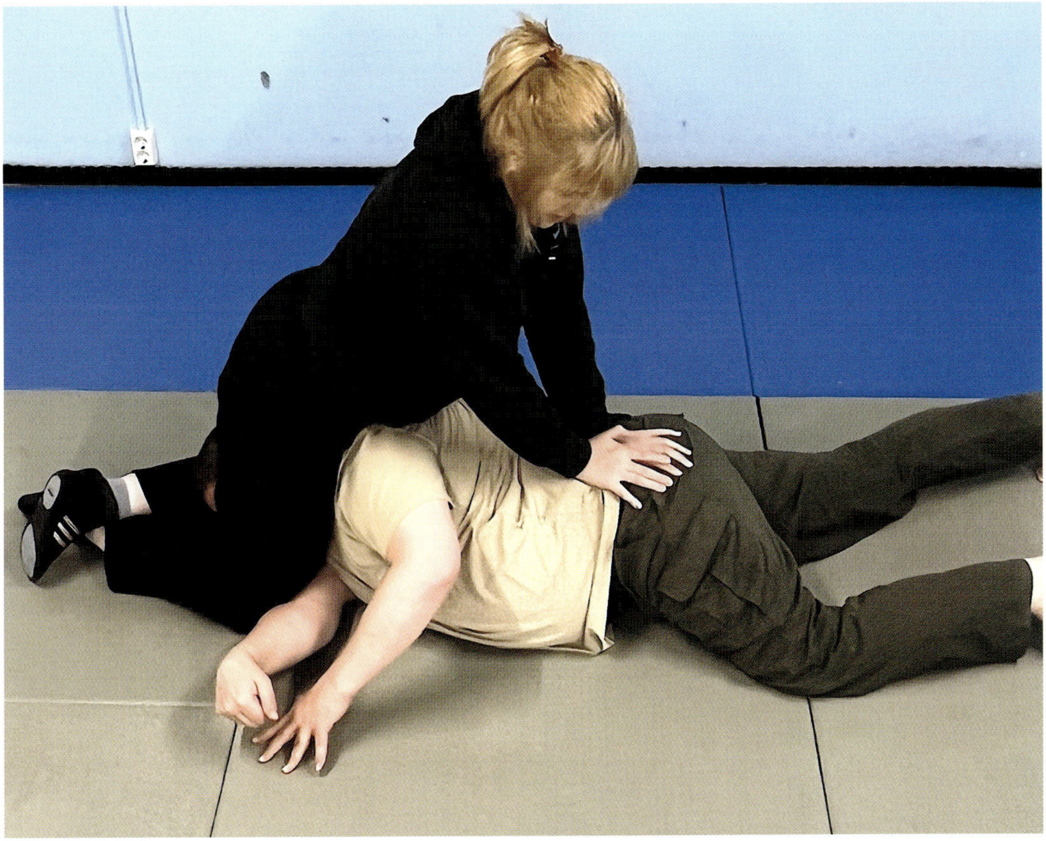

Pinning the attacker down with her hips and hands, the defender can now get up and move out.

Attacker's intention: pinning with a side headlock

If the attacker manages to establish a better headlock and get the defender's hand under control, there is a brief window to counter, since the attacker can't stay in that position very long. He will either try to get the defender's shoulder to lock and break or move to a better position to start striking.

Attacker's intention: close in

One further basic situation involving the use of headlocks on the ground has the attacker squeezing in and using both their arm and shoulder to pin the defender down.

The attacker is squeezing in tightly, making it difficult for the defender.

The defender needs to move her hips out quickly, simultaneously using a hook-type punch to hit the attacker's head fast to the ground. Repeat the punch for every inch of the turn she needs to make.

Using the momentum from the punches, the defender keeps on turning and pushing the attacker's head apart from his shoulder, so restricting the power from his biceps to curl back in.

By using her bodyweight against the attacker's arm, the defender creates a shoulder lock to either detain the attacker or break his arm, so enabling her to escape.

REAR-NAKED CHOKE ON THE GROUND

We learned earlier how to defend against a rear-naked choke while standing. We'll now move on to dealing with a situation in which that hold brings us down to the ground. Once the defender perceives that her balance is gone, she must revert to going along with the result and start defending on the ground.

There is a high probability that the attacker will try to close his legs and prevent the defender from doing the roll backwards. Should this happen, the key factor is to move one's body in a sliding motion upwards towards the attacker's face and start turning while doing this. Don't get too distracted by the pinning legs, as the true problem is the choking hand. It is very important to prevent the attacker pressing down the defender's hips while squeezing the neck.

The attacker is taking the defender to the ground.

As the attacker keeps on pulling backwards, the defender needs to use that movement to her advantage by rolling backwards over the attacker, so releasing herself.

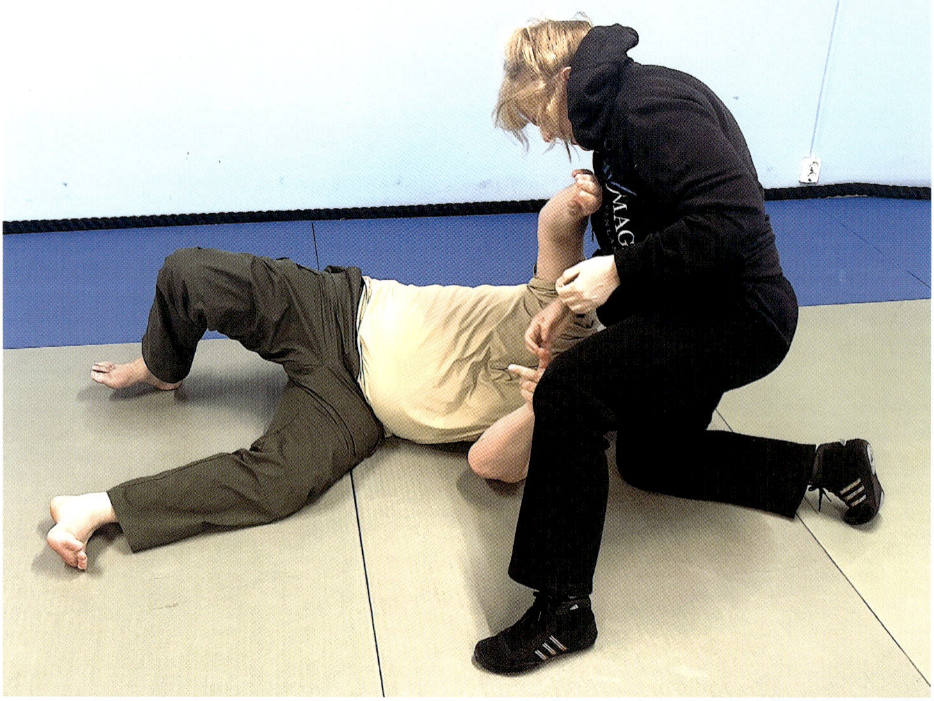

Getting her feet on the ground, the defender is able to free herself from the headlock and do what is needed to get away.

The attacker has locked his legs around the defender and is trying to pin her hips straight and pull her neck up to keep the strangulation fast and furious.

Breaking the attacker's structure by pushing her head higher, while keeping her neck tucked in for protection, the defender breaks the leg lock.

By kicking and turning while continuing to push the attacker's head back with her own head, the defender is rolling towards escape as before.

SUMMARY

The ground is one of the hardest environments on which to defend oneself. The surface, the space and all the sharp angles, the unevenness and other factors, not to mention the strength and weight differences of the participants, make it extremely challenging. We seldom have an opportunity to train in such environments but once we do, safety becomes an ever more important factor. There are so many more variations to consider than when training on a mat. Nevertheless, ground defence is a very important aspect of self-defence and should be integrated into the representative practice design.

In the final chapter we'll investigate high-threat situations, exploring how the basic movement solutions are applied in these situations.

14 HIGH-THREAT SITUATIONS

Self-defence situations are far from clinical and controlled. This is especially true when the attacker may be armed with blunt objects, edged weapons or firearms, or there are multiple attackers. Time and distance are everything. This is why we must treat every situation from the mindset that there might be weapons of some sort and perhaps more than one attacker.

THERE IS NO SUCH THING AS KNIFE DEFENCE

It is said that the majority of those who have been stabbed never even saw the knife. That's why we can also say that there is no such thing as knife defence, just defence. I faced a situation with a knife a few times during my days in operative security. On one occasion the knife was plainly in sight and I was able to talk that situation down before the police took charge. Other times the person tried to hit me, but I only found he had a knife when he was already in custody or been overpowered before they had the time to take it out. The combat mindset was then at high alert, after all I was working. These were no surprises, white- or even yellow-stage situations. Everything was orange, red and then action.

REACTION OR DECISION

We have covered the basic tactics and principles of self-defence. It is very important to make a distinction between reacting to an incoming attack or deciding to act upon a threat. If someone takes out a firearm or any other weapon with the intention of threatening you, they have the power. In these situations we are dealing with decision-making, not necessarily reacting. Use the Distraction, Disabling, Detaining and Disappearing principle or persuade the person to calm down with communication. That is the decision we'll need to make before taking further action. That is where the situational awareness framework comes into play, taking the situation towards a solution where we have time to flee. Choose safety. Sometimes de-escalation means taking the person out and sometimes talking them down.

FIREARMS

Scrolling through the internet there are hundreds of mechanical solutions to threats from firearms. Evidence from CCTV shows that the combat mindset is the most important thing. If a person holding the firearm isn't really prepared to use it, while the defender is equipped to rip their head off, the ripper usually survives. There are also situations in which the defender has started to act and made a miscalculation: and the firearm-holder responds by shooting. If you use pellet guns or other pain-bullet providers when training, you will conclude that distraction, disabling, detaining works. If you try to go in without distraction and your training partner is ready to fire, the little red dots on your body will serve as a reminder. Remember to wear safety goggles all the time you're near the projectile-sending equipment. The real question we need to keep asking is whether the training situations truly represent reality.

I vividly remember a news item in the Finnish newspaper *Helsingin Sanomat* during the 1980s: 'four hooligans attacked a WW2 veteran, one of them got away'. That veteran obviously wasn't choosing to just defend himself since lions don't block. He just did what he had obviously done before in the trenches and forests in the 1940s. This is the combat mindset. Once you see that there is no escape, start attacking or, as Imi Lichtenfeld said, 'don't get hurt but if you do, keep on fighting'. The key principle here is a simple matter of customer service practice: put them in a line and deal with them one at a time. Situational awareness can help us avoid this, but if we make a mistake, by training to be a lion our time may come.

CLOSING WORDS

Writing this book has been very inspiring. It has also taken a lot of effort and still there is so much to say about the years I've spent training and coaching, finding answers to how to acquire skills and be ready anywhere and anytime. I knew it would be about teaching and learning. The dilemma of training one way and then rising to the situation by totally differently methods has bothered me from the start. But for the first ten years or so I drilled and drilled and gained practical experience, before translating my friends' and my own experiences into technical exercises, integrating psychology with physiology. But something was still missing. Finally, I understood that it was more about behaviour than engineering.

About 2008 I started looking at ways of teaching and training Krav Maga, and the other zero-distance solutions I coach and teach in the security and military, from the aspect of human behaviour rather than techniques. I had no original theory behind it, just practice and assumptions backed up by behavioural science but not linked to zero-distance movement performance. The schema theory was there, but it really didn't prove itself without the ecological dynamics and the CLA. Information processing and linear pedagogy had always been there, but never really worked as a way of quickly transferring the necessary skills. With time, of course, everything works and the more time you commit to resistance training, sparring, in different environments and with different people, the more you will learn.

In 2019 I discovered the ecological dynamics theory and CLA and the picture became clear. Now we have a systematic form of nonlinear pedagogy, the system being that the coaches need to create the exercises individually in a group. It is now my mission to help every instructor and coach to teach by using ecological dynamics, create skill adaptation by using CLA and naturally help everyone learn how to defend oneself in an ever-motivating way. The learning never ends, and we can always be better, since safe failures lead to higher skill.

I truly hope you have enjoyed this book and all the material included. I have tried my best to give you my experience on what and how to train to stay out of trouble or, should the trouble still find you or those close to you, to survive that day. As the saying goes, experience is something we get after we need it. By practising and experiencing self-defence, we can gain some of that experience beforehand. We know that it will never be the same as in training, but let's do all we can to live to tell the tale and share our experiences with others. Remember that the vision of Imi Lichtenfeld, the founder of Krav Maga, was that it was intended 'so that one could walk in peace'.

INDEX

First published in 2026 by
The Crowood Press Ltd
Ramsbury, Marlborough
Wiltshire SN8 2HR

enquiries@crowood.com
www.crowood.com

British Library Cataloguing-in-Publication Data
A catalogue record for this book is available from the British Library.

For product safety-related questions, contact: productsafety@crowood.com

ISBN 978 0 7198 4630 4

Disclaimer

The information provided in this book is intended for general knowledge and informational purposes only. It is not a substitute for professional medical advice, diagnosis, or treatment. Always seek the advice of your doctor or other qualified healthcare provider with any questions you may have regarding a medical condition or before starting any new exercise, fitness, or dietary programme.

Performing the exercises or utilising any information contained in this book is done at your own risk. Neither the author nor the publisher shall be held liable for any injuries, health issues, or damages resulting from the use of this book. By using this book, you agree to assume full responsibility for any and all injuries or damages that may occur, and you expressly waive any claims against the author or publisher arising from your use of the information or exercises contained herein.

Typeset by Envisage IT

Cover design by Catherine Murray

Printed and bound in India by Parksons Graphics Pvt Ltd

ACKNOWLEDGEMENTS

This book would not have been possible without the inspiration and encouragement of my coach and spouse Hedi Viisma. The hours spent taking almost a thousand photographs, assessing the set-ups and angles, and repeatedly redoing some of them, while bouncing ideas about faster ways of teaching and learning, has been so valuable that I truly wish everyone could have the same kind of support and love in their life. Thank you, my love!

The list of my teachers, colleagues and peers is long, but I want to thank you all for your advice and example. I wouldn't be on this path without the guidance of Soke Auvo Niiniketo, the founder of Hokutoryu jujutsu and a key figure in so many martial arts in Finland. Kudos also to my Krav Maga teachers, GM Eyal Yanilov, with whom I started my instructor career in 2000, GM Avi Abeceedon, the head of the martial arts section of the Levinsky-Wingate Academic College, and GM Raphy Elgrissy, a true legend who has been a constant example of what it means to be humble while learning from everyone. The list goes on with my dear friends and colleagues Ron Rotem, Danny Netzer and Amit Porat. Everyone at the Federation of Israeli Martial Arts community (www.thefima.com) should be named here. I must also give my sincerest appreciation to an astonishing coach, Tony Blauer.

I also want to thank all the people with whom I train. Without the endless hours spent together sharing ideas, expertise and acquiring new skills I could not become a better coach and version of myself. Thank you!